The Blended Learning Blueprint for Elementary Teachers

For Ken, who would have been the first to read it.

The Blended Learning Blueprint for Elementary Teachers

Jayme Linton

CORWIN
A SAGE Publishing Company

FOR INFORMATION:

Corwin

A SAGE Company

2455 Teller Road

Thousand Oaks, California 91320

(800) 233-9936

www.corwin.com

SAGE Publications Ltd.

1 Oliver's Yard

55 City Road

London EC1Y 1SP

United Kingdom

SAGE Publications India Pvt. Ltd.

B 1/I 1 Mohan Cooperative Industrial Area

Mathura Road, New Delhi 110 044

India

SAGE Publications Asia-Pacific Pte. Ltd.

3 Church Street

#10-04 Samsung Hub

Singapore 049483

Acquisitions Editor: Ariel Curry

Development Editor: Desirée A. Bartlett

Editorial Assistant: Jessica Vidal

Production Editor: Tori Mirsadjadi

Copy Editor: Robin Gold

Typesetter: C&M Digitals (P) Ltd.

Proofreader: Talia Greenberg

Indexer: Wendy Allex

Cover Designer: Candice Harman

Marketing Manager: Margaret O'Connor

Printed in the United States of America

Library of Congress Cataloging-in-Publication Data

Names: Linton, Jayme, author.

Title: The blended learning blueprint for elementary teachers / Jayme Linton.

Description: Thousand Oaks, Calif. : Corwin, 2018. | Includes bibliographical references and index.

Identifiers: LCCN 2017045272 | ISBN 9781544318639 (pbk. : alk. paper)

Subjects: LCSH: Education, Elementary—United States. | Education, Elementary—Computer-assisted instruction. | Blended learning—United States.

Classification: LCC LA219 .L56 2018 | DDC 371.3—dc23

LC record available at https://lccn.loc.gov/2017045272

This book is printed on acid-free paper.

SUSTAINABLE FORESTRY INITIATIVE

Certified Chain of Custody

At Least 10% Certified Forest Content

www.sfiprogram.org

SFI-01028

20 21 22 10 9 8 7 6 5 4 3 2

Contents

Preface

Rationale

Districts, schools, and teachers are turning to blended learning as a way to leverage devices for student success. Although fully brick-and-mortar and fully virtual learning environments offer benefits to various types of learners, a blend of face-to-face and online learning opportunities has the potential to increase K–12 student learning and engagement. This is particularly true in elementary classrooms, where students and their families typically have fewer options beyond the brick-and-mortar school. Blended learning enables teachers to take advantage of the affordances of technology while increasing the impact of face-to-face instruction. Through purposeful design and facilitation of face-to-face and online learning experiences, teachers can meet the needs of each learner and manage personalized learning pathways for students.

School districts tend to focus their technology efforts (funds, professional development, and policies) on high school students to equip them for their futures in higher education and the workforce. Programs that involve purchasing a device for every student (1-to-1) or enable students to bring devices from home (BYOD) tend to be targeted at our oldest K–12 students. This leads elementary teachers to seek out their own solutions for leveraging technology to shift teaching and learning in their classrooms.

I argue that blended learning is a natural fit for the elementary classroom, where many teachers already think flexibly about the learning environment, resources, and time in order to meet diverse student needs. However, making the shift to blended learning requires intentional planning and support. As more and more classrooms become settings for blended learning, teachers and school and district leaders need to develop a shared understanding of the characteristics of effective instruction in blended environments. Blended learning involves more than simply adding devices to a traditional classroom model. However, in many schools implementing blended learning, the conversation quickly shifts to devices while overlooking the essential foundations of a blended learning environment.

The goal of this book is to help guide elementary teachers through the transition toward blended learning, focusing on support for the most critical component of an effective blended environment: the teacher.

This book aims to help elementary educators working in or transitioning toward blended settings develop a blueprint for successful implementation of blended learning in their classrooms.

Organization

The iNACOL Blended Learning Teacher Competency Framework, a framework outlining the characteristics of successful blended teachers, provides a common lens and shared language for this book. The first chapter of the book provides an in-depth look at the competency framework to foster a deeper understanding of the teacher competencies needed for effective blended learning environments. As teachers read Chapter 1, they will identify their own strengths and needs related to the blended teacher competencies.

The remainder of the book serves as a guide to support teachers through a successful transition to blended instruction. Teachers will be guided through the development of a blueprint for designing and facilitating blended learning in their classrooms. This book will serve as a workbook, providing strategies and examples of blended learning in elementary classrooms along with opportunities for teachers to design and reflect on their own plans for blended instruction. This format will make visible the instructional decisions of effective blended teachers, helping make quality blended instruction transparent and actionable.

Features of each chapter focus on blended learning in action, including images, lesson plans, student work samples, and digital resources.

Readers will be able to

- Reflect on the competencies needed for effective blended instruction

- Explore strategies and methods for blended learning environments

- Design a blueprint for implementing blended learning in their classrooms

- Evaluate and reflect on instruction in their own blended contexts

This book aims to take the mystery out of effective blended teaching and provide a guide to support elementary teachers in designing and facilitating blended learning. By crafting a blueprint, readers will design their own personalized implementation plans for blended learning.

Possible Uses

This guidebook is designed to help K–5 teachers develop and carry out a plan for effective instruction in blended environments. Serving as a step-by-step guide, this book will present the competencies blended teachers need and strategies for developing those competencies and prompt teachers to develop a personalized implementation plan for successful blended instruction. Elementary teachers and school and district leaders could use this book to assist with the design and facilitation of quality blended learning experiences. In addition to supporting individual teachers in developing competencies for blended learning, schools and districts can use this book to develop a shared understanding of quality blended learning environments and work collaboratively to leverage blended methods for student learning.

Educators who provide professional development for elementary teachers, including instructional technology facilitators, instructional coaches, and others, could use this book to design face-to-face, blended, and online professional development for blended teachers. Each section of the book could be the focus of a professional development session. Professional development providers could use the book as a guide during hands-on, application-based professional development as teachers create or redesign blended learning opportunities based on ideas and resources provided in the book.

University instructors could use this book as required or suggested reading in courses focused on blended teaching methods. In those courses, undergraduate and graduate students could use the book as a guide to complete course assignments and apply effective blended teaching methods in their coursework, blended teaching practica, and K–12 blended learning environments.

Acknowledgments

This book would not be possible without the inspiration, effort, and support of many incredible educators. Thank you to the teachers and administrators at the Shuford School of Blended Learning in Newton-Conover City Schools and Oakwood Elementary in Hickory Public Schools. I would especially like to thank Jessica Fitzgerald, Melissa White, and Caitlan Reese for welcoming me into their classrooms and their principals, Patrick Nelson and Dr. Jennifer Griffin, who supported this project. Thanks also to Tammy Brown, Stacey Mrazek, and Dr. David Stegall for their contributions and support. I'm grateful that my children, along with many others, have benefited from the passion, talent, and hard work of the educators featured in this book.

I also owe a debt of gratitude to my colleagues in the School of Education at Lenoir-Rhyne University who tirelessly support preservice teachers and who have improved the quality of learning for students in so many classrooms. They constantly raise the bar for teaching and learning, and I am grateful to be among them. Go Bears!

No amount of effort on my part would have been sufficient to lead to the publication of this book without the support and constant encouragement of my family. My mother, Lynne Morris, has been my cheerleader and my editor for many years, and she continues to challenge me to be better as an educator, a scholar, and a person. My husband, Angelos, makes what I do possible. Thank you for giving me time to write. Thanks also to my sweet Annie and Deacon, who make me prouder than anything else in my life. I'm so blessed to be your mom.

Publisher's Acknowledgments

Corwin gratefully acknowledges the following reviewers for their editorial insight and guidance:

Tamara Daugherty, Fourth-Grade Teacher
Zellwood Elementary
Zellwood, Florida

Kendra Hanzlik, Instructional Coach
Prairie Hill Elementary
Cedar Rapids, Iowa

Tanna Nicely, Executive Principal
South Knoxville Elementary
Knoxville, Tennessee

About the Author

Dr. Jayme Linton is Assistant Professor of Education at Lenoir-Rhyne University in Hickory, North Carolina. Jayme is married to a high-energy husband and mom to two fun-loving children, ages ten and six. Jayme developed and coordinates Lenoir-Rhyne's graduate program in online teaching and instructional design. She received her PhD in teacher education from the University of North Carolina at Greensboro, a bachelor's degree in elementary education from Western Carolina University, and a master's degree in curriculum and instruction from Appalachian State University. Previously, she held positions as instructional technology facilitator, staff development coordinator, instructional coach, and elementary teacher. She was recognized by the National School Board Association as one of the "20 to Watch" for 2012–2013 and was selected for the International Society for Technology in Education (ISTE)'s Making IT Happen Award by the North Carolina Technology in Education Society (NCTIES) in 2013. Her research and professional learning focus on preparation and support for online instructors, online and blended learning communities for educators, blended learning in K–12, personal learning networks for preservice teachers, and professional learning for technology integration.

Introduction

Defining Blended Learning

Why Blended Learning?

Technology affords new opportunities for teaching and learning, including the ability to personalize instruction for each student, measure student progress with real-time data, provide immediate feedback, and adjust instruction based on student learning needs. One of the greatest benefits of technology in today's classrooms is its ability to enable teachers to be more responsive to students. No longer must teachers wait until the end of the unit, the end of the day, or the end of the lesson to determine how well students are progressing toward learning outcomes and make adjustments to instruction.

More so, blended learning is a method that enables teachers to transform learning for students. In this book, blended learning will be presented not as the goal but as a means to an end. As you will see, the ultimate goal of blended learning is personalized, equitable learning experiences for all students. Blended learning can remove barriers to equity and allow each student control over the where, when, and how of their own learning. As you work to sharpen your own skills as a blended teacher, keep in mind that blended learning serves as a way to meet the needs of all learners. Implementing blended learning well is not the goal. However, to leverage blended learning to achieve equity and personalization, teachers must first develop specific blended learning competencies and think strategically about the resources, tools, and strategies at their disposal. This leads us to the purpose of this book: to equip teachers with the competencies needed to design and facilitate blended learning that enables personalized and equitable learning experiences for students.

Blended learning acknowledges the indispensable role of the teacher in facilitating student learning while acknowledging the advantages of technology applications on student learning. For example, technology can make data collection and analysis more efficient, provide learning experiences that adapt based on student responses, and allow students to control the pace and place of their learning. Teachers, then, can respond to student needs with targeted instruction, design real-world opportunities for students to apply their learning, and provide personalized feedback to help each student progress toward learning outcomes. In other words, in blended settings, teachers let technology do what it's good at so that they can do what they're good at.

> Blended learning serves as a way to meet the needs of all learners.

As you read this book and work through each section of the blended learning blueprint, you will learn more about how to leverage technology to reap the many benefits of blended learning, such as

- Increased instructional time
- Personalized learning opportunities for students
- Student empowerment and engagement
- Collaborative learning opportunities
- Student-paced and student-led learning
- Increased opportunities for student voice

It is important to clarify that blended learning is not about technology. Rather, blended learning, as you will see in this book, involves a shift in how we think about teaching and learning. Although technology is a tool that enables blended learning, teachers in blended classrooms can attest that effective blended instruction is about more than mastering new tools. Successful blended instruction depends on thoughtful and intentional planning, design, and facilitation by the teacher.

Definition and Models of Blended Learning

A quick Google search will reveal many different definitions of *blended learning*, each including some element of face-to-face and online instruction. Definitions that simplify blended learning as any form of instruction that includes face-to-face and online instruction overlook the purpose of blended learning. For that reason, I prefer the following definition from the Christensen Institute because of its focus on blended learning as a method to achieve personalized learning.

The definition of *blended learning* is "a formal education program in which a student learns:

- at least in part through online learning, with some element of student control over time, place, path, and/or pace;

- at least in part in a supervised brick-and-mortar location away from home;

- and the modalities along each student's learning path within a course or subject are connected to provide an integrated learning experience." (Horn & Staker, 2014)

I would like to pause here for a moment to further explore this definition. By examining each element of this definition individually, we are able to better glimpse the complexity and the purpose of blended learning. Consider each of the following elements of blended learning in Table 0.1.

When I work with teachers, coaches, and administrators around blended learning, I often ask them to analyze this definition, piece by piece, as I have done here. The purpose of this activity is to encourage educators to reflect and self-assess, identifying which elements of blended learning are in place in their contexts and which are opportunities for growth. I encourage you to take time now to reflect on each element of the Christensen definition. Use Table 0.1 to jot down your reflections. Which components of blended learning are strengths of your instructional

Table 0.1 Blended Learning Defined

Elements of Blended Learning	Your Reflections
A student learns at least in part through online learning	
with some element of control over time, place, path, and/or pace;	
at least in part in a supervised brick-and-mortar location away from home;	
and the modalities along each student's learning path within a course or subject are connected to provide an integrated learning experience.	

approach? Which components offer opportunities for growth? As you explore blended instructional strategies throughout this book, use your self-assessment to assist you in identifying the changes in practice that can help you implement each element of this definition.

Now that you have a working definition of *blended learning*, let's turn our attention to blended learning models. Endless possibilities exist for how blended learning can be designed and implemented. Although we will explore a few agreed-upon blended models in this Introduction, blended learning is essentially a continuum from mostly face-to-face to mostly online instruction. These models can provide a common language for educators; however, keep in mind that any given model can be implemented differently from school to school and from classroom to classroom.

The Christensen Institute has identified and defined four main models of blended learning. Again, these models can provide a common language and help teachers and administrators envision what blended learning might look like in their classrooms and schools. The four models identified by the Christensen Institute are presented in Table 0.2.

The flex, à la carte, and enriched virtual models are primarily used in high schools to provide students with flexibility, choice, and access to courses they might not have at their local schools. Each of those three models relies heavily on stand-alone online courses as a supplement to traditional face-to-face courses. The four rotation models, however, are most common in elementary schools and arguably most appropriate for the elementary student, so we will focus on those here. To help you envision each of these models in an elementary classroom and evaluate their usefulness, I have provided a closer look at the four rotation models in Table 0.3. For the sake of comparison, each model is described with a focus on elementary math. However, keep in mind that these models are appropriate for any content area.

As a blended elementary teacher, you do not have to choose one model over the others. You may like certain aspects of one model but prefer different aspects of another. In a real classroom, blended learning typically takes shape as a combination of these different models. Think flexibly about the models, and choose the pieces that work best for you and your students. One model might work better for some units of study, or a different model might be a better fit at certain times of the school year.

One word of caution: an emphasis on models of implementation can lead to the false notion that effective blended instruction is all about implementing a model well. As we will explore in Chapter 1, effective blended instruction requires that teachers possess specific competencies to design, facilitate, and lead blended learning in an effort to increase equity and personalization.

> Blended learning typically takes shape as a combination of these different models.

Table 0.2 Blended Learning Models

Blended Learning Continuum	Model	Definition
Mostly Face-to-Face ↑ ↓ Mostly Online	Rotation Model	The most common blended learning model in elementary and middle schools, the rotation model involves students rotating on a fixed schedule among face-to-face and online learning experiences designed by the teacher. These rotations can take place within a single classroom or across multiple classrooms. The rotation model has four common formats: a. Station Rotation—The station rotation model involves students rotating through multiple stations, with each student rotating to every station. b. Lab Rotation—The lab rotation model involves students rotating to a lab classroom for online instruction. c. Flipped Classroom—The flipped classroom model uses online learning to deliver content to students outside of the classroom, typically for homework, but face-to-face instruction and interaction occur in the classroom. d. Individual Rotation—The individual rotation model involves students rotating through face-to-face and online learning stations according to individualized playlists.
	Flex Model	Through the flex model, students learn primarily through online instruction, although students engage with this instruction mostly in a brick-and-mortar school. Online instruction may sometimes direct students to off-line experiences. The on-site instructor-of-record is available to supplement online instruction flexibly as needed.
	À La Carte Model	The à la carte model allows students to take an entirely online course as part of their overall learning experience. These students may complete online coursework at a school or away from school. The online instructor is the instructor of record, but an on-site facilitator might provide technical assistance.
	Enriched Virtual Model	Most instruction in an enriched virtual model occurs away from a school, and online learning is the primary method of instruction. The online instructor-of-record may occasionally require on-site sessions, although students primarily work asynchronously and at a distance from the instructor.

Source: Horn, M. B., & Staker, H. (2014). *Blended: Using disruptive innovation to improve schools.* San Francisco, CA: Jossey-Bass.

Internet Safety in the Elementary Classroom

Teachers in all elementary classrooms, particularly blended classrooms, should become familiar with federal rules and regulations for children's Internet safety along with their local school district's policies related to children's online activity. Two major federal acts provide protection for children online. The Children's Internet Protection Act (CIPA) requires that schools and libraries implement Internet safety policies and precautions, including filtering or blocking harmful online content. Schools must

Table 0.3 Rotation Models in a Blended Elementary Classroom

	Example in Elementary Math	Benefits	Limitations
Station Rotation	In mixed-ability groups that change weekly based on pre-assessment data, students rotate through four different math stations each day. Two stations involve working with manipulatives to solve problems. At the other two stations, students work online using adaptive programs such as Khan Academy and online skill practice sites. The teacher pulls students from across the four groups to teach targeted skill lessons based on formative assessment data.	Elementary teachers who already use stations in the classroom can easily transition to this model, which supports collaborative learning and provides time for small-group instruction.	In a typical station rotation model, all students rotate through the same stations. With this model, there is less flexibility to adapt the learning experience for each individual student.
Lab Rotation	As a class works on a collaborative project involving measurement and geometry, students complete most of their project work in the classroom. However, the class visits the school's computer lab once or twice a week to work through virtual simulations of the project. The teacher schedules lab time at purposeful times throughout the project.	This model works well in classrooms where students have limited access to devices. Intentional planning can help students maximize time available in the lab.	This model limits time available for students and teacher to leverage technology for personalized learning, relying more heavily on face-to-face instruction.
Flipped Classroom	For homework, students watch teacher-created videos demonstrating how to solve multistep word problems using a variety of examples. In class, students work in collaborative groups to solve multistep problems, applying strategies learned from the teacher-created videos. The teacher provides small-group and individual instruction and support as needed.	Flipped learning maximizes time on task by using technology for content delivery outside of the regular school day. Class time is used for interaction, active learning, and teacher feedback.	The flipped learning model depends on students having access to content outside of the classroom. Not all students have this kind of access readily available.
Individual Rotation	Students select math tasks from their personalized learning pathways (more in Chapter 4) and work through those tasks at their own pace. Some tasks involve the use of digital tools, but others do not. The teacher designs the pathways and provides just-in-time support for students through small-group lessons, whole-group mini-lessons, and individual conferences.	The individual rotation model provides the greatest flexibility for personalized learning and student control over time, place, path, and pace.	Transitioning to this model requires significant shifts in how we think about teaching and learning and can be very time-intensive.

agree to monitor children's online activity and teach children about appropriate and safe online behavior. This protection is provided at the school or district level.

The Children's Online Privacy Protection Act (COPPA) regulates websites and online services aimed at children younger than thirteen years of age or websites that knowingly collect personal information from children younger than thirteen years old. Under COPPA guidelines, parental consent is required before a website can collect personal information from children under the age of thirteen. Many school districts have a list of approved websites that are safe for children and do not collect personal information. If you have not seen such a list, ask for one. To use any sites not on an approved district list, you may be directed by district administration to get parental permission first.

If your students' parents and families have concerns about Internet safety in a blended classroom, you can direct them to ftc.gov to learn more about how these regulations protect their children. Some schools and districts have invested time in educating parents about Internet safety and tips they can use at home. This is a tremendous resource for parents and can be a great opportunity to work with families as partners in their children's education. I also encourage you to seek out your district's policies related to Internet use and share these with your students' families. Ultimately, you must respect the students' families and comply with their requests.

If families are concerned about children's online activity in your blended classroom, transparency is often the best policy. Invite families to your classroom to see how students use online resources and tools, and share with them a list of all the sites their children will be using. Consider hosting a family night to provide information about blended learning and allow time for students to show their families how they use devices as part of their overall learning experience.

In this Introduction, we have examined a few of the fundamental elements of a blended elementary classroom. Let's now turn our attention to the single most important factor in the blended classroom: the teacher. In Chapter 1, we will explore the competencies teachers need for success in a blended learning environment.

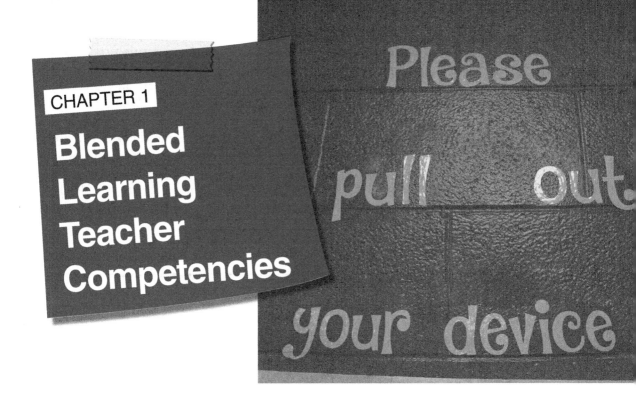

CHAPTER 1

Blended Learning Teacher Competencies

The International Association for K–12 Online Learning has developed a set of competencies for teachers called the Blended Learning Teacher Competency Framework. This framework can guide teachers and school and district leaders as they work to build capacity for effective blended instruction. Successful blended teachers must develop critical competencies (mindsets, qualities, and skills) that allow them to leverage technology and face-to-face instruction to meet the needs of all learners.

This chapter introduces the iNACOL Blended Learning Teacher Competency Framework, which includes the key characteristics—the mindsets, qualities, and skills—of teachers in successful blended environments. These competencies, identified by leading experts in the field of blended and online learning, provide a vision for a well-equipped blended learning teacher. Rather than emphasizing blended models or strategies, this framework gets at the heart of successful blended learning: the competent teacher. As you read this chapter, you may realize that these competencies are not restricted to blended teachers alone. You could argue that these competencies are mindsets, qualities, and skills that all teachers should possess. However, as this framework clearly describes, these competencies are absolutely essential for successful blended learning environments.

Although the remaining chapters serve as a practical guidebook for elementary blended teachers, I would argue that this is the single most important chapter in the book. A successful transition to blended learning requires that teachers become familiar with certain instructional strategies and tools and develop the necessary mindsets, qualities, and skills for blended instruction. This chapter provides an overview of those competencies, and Appendix C offers you an opportunity to reflect on your strengths and identify areas for growth. The remaining chapters will provide strategies and examples of these competencies in action. Beginning with this framework allows us to keep our focus on the elementary classroom teacher before diving into specific components of an effective blended learning approach.

Mindsets

> Competency 1: New vision for teaching and learning
>
> Competency 2: Orientation toward change and improvement

Successful blended learning initiatives begin with a shift in mindset. Rather than adapting current teaching and learning structures or injecting technology into our existing practices, we must begin by envisioning anew what teaching and learning could look like in an elementary blended setting. Without changing mindsets to embrace a new vision for teaching and learning and an orientation toward continuous improvement, blended learning initiatives fall short of our expectations for student achievement and transformative learning experiences. The iNACOL Blended Learning Teacher Competency Framework identifies two essential mindsets for the blended teacher: a new vision for teaching and learning and an orientation toward change and improvement.

The fact that iNACOL lists the mindset competency first in the Blended Learning Teacher Competency Framework should get our attention. To be successful in a blended learning environment, teachers need to possess or develop the right mindsets. The first, and most critical, mindset is a new vision for teaching and learning. Too many blended learning initiatives fail because they begin with devices, models, or instructional strategies. Although those things are important, they could be misplaced or misused if we fail to begin with a new vision for teaching and learning. To carry out a new vision for teaching and learning, teachers must be open to change and continuous improvement. An orientation toward change and improvement enables a new vision to take shape and become a reality. We will take a closer look at continuous improvement in the blended elementary classroom in Chapter 7.

Qualities

Competency 1: Grit

Competency 2: Transparency

Competency 3: Collaboration

Master blended learning teachers possess the qualities of grit, transparency, and collaboration. Whereas the mindsets for successful blended teaching must be understood, adopted, and committed to, these qualities must be coached, encouraged, and reinforced. Teachers can help each other develop and strengthen these qualities through peer coaching and encouragement. Additionally, through frequent reflection and goal-setting, teachers can identify strengths and areas for improvement and implement plans of action to strengthen their grit, transparency, and collaboration.

If you are a blended elementary teacher, you already recognize the role of grit in designing, facilitating, and managing blended learning experiences. Change is hard, and things won't always go well the first time around. Thankfully, working with a team of educators who are passionate and committed to successful blended learning can be a tremendous asset. Transparency involves a willingness to share your practice openly with others and analyze your practice objectively. It can be uncomfortable sharing our practice openly when our colleagues have very different visions for teaching and learning. However, transparency within a community of educators can serve as a catalyst for growth and improvement of our practice and, ultimately, the success of our students. As a blended teacher, you know that you can't do this difficult and transformative work alone. Collaboration is a key blended teacher competency, honoring the fact that teachers must depend on and support one another as well as reach out beyond their schools to connect with others who can support them in this work.

Adaptive Skills

Competency 1: Reflection

Competency 2: Continuous Improvement and Innovation

Competency 3: Communication

Functioning day in and day out in a blended learning environment requires flexibility and adaptability. We must become more flexible in the ways we think about the role of the teacher, the role of the student, our use of time, and the design of the learning environment. Adaptive skills for the blended teacher include reflection, continuous improvement and innovation, and communication. According to the iNACOL Blended Learning Teacher Competency Framework, these adaptive skills can be developed through modeling, coaching, and reflective practice.

Collaborative and change-oriented conversations about the best use of face-to-face and online learning can happen in professional learning community (PLC) meetings, faculty meetings, coaching sessions, and planning meetings. During these conversations, everyone must be willing to set aside preconceptions and embrace some uncertainty. If we each approach the blended learning transition thinking we have everything figured out, we won't get very far with implementing a new vision for teaching and learning. We must be open to thinking about new possibilities without shutting down ideas that seem unclear at first but could radically affect student learning.

Technical Skills

Competency 1: Data Practices

Competency 2: Instructional Strategies

Competency 3: Management of the Blended Learning Experience

Competency 4: Instructional Tools

Although blended learning is not solely about using blended strategies and tools, we do know that the purposeful use of specific instructional strategies and technologies are a big part of what makes blended learning "blended." To be effective in a blended elementary classroom, teachers need to possess certain technical skills related to data, instruction, management, and technology. These technical skills tend to be the first competencies we think about when we consider what blended teachers need to know and be able to do. However, it is worth noting that iNACOL places these competencies at the very end of the Blended Learning Teacher Competency Framework. These skills are essential for a successful blended classroom, but they should be developed along with the right mindsets, qualities, and adaptive skills. Teachers can master these technical skills through instruction, training, and practice.

Data practices, instructional strategies, management skills, and fluency with instructional tools make up a blended teacher's day-to-day work. These are the nitty-gritty nuts and bolts that make a blended classroom run smoothly, and they are the skills that enable teachers to leverage technology to transform learning possibilities for students. Remember that our goals for implementing blended learning involve increasing personalization, empowerment, and equity for students. The technical skills identified by the iNACOL framework are the means toward that end.

> Our goals for implementing blended learning involve increasing personalization, empowerment, and equity for students.

The Blended Learning Teacher Competency Framework provides an in-depth look at the mindsets, qualities, and skills needed for success in a blended learning environment. Each of the competencies presented in this framework exists as a continuum, with teachers ranging from novice to accomplished. None of us have mastered all of these competencies. The goal for you is to identify your own areas of strength and opportunities for improvement and to take steps forward along the continuum.

The remaining chapters in this book will present ways of thinking, strategies, and tools for success in the blended elementary classroom. Based on your reflections from this chapter, you can determine which sections of this book will support you the most in developing these blended learning teacher competencies. Each chapter includes one piece of a blueprint, which will guide you and help you consider ways to apply what you learn to your own classroom. The full blueprint can be found in Appendix A. Together, your blended competency reflections and your completed blueprint will provide a clear guide for your next steps in implementing blended learning effectively.

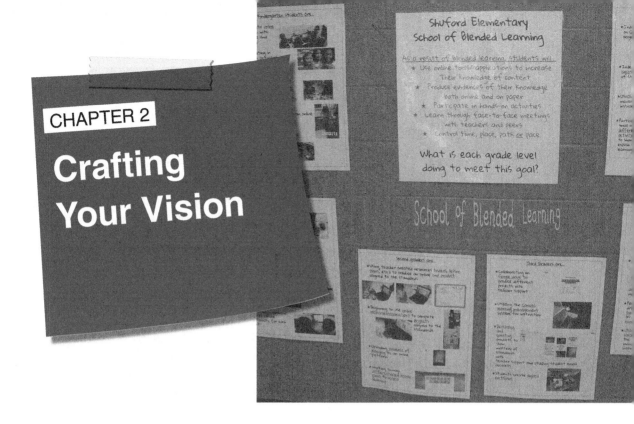

CHAPTER 2
Crafting Your Vision

In this chapter, we will consider the following elements of a vision for blended learning:

- Adapting blended models
- Rethinking the role of teachers and learners
- Letting go of control
- Redesigning the learning space

By the end of this chapter, you will be able to complete the *Crafting Your Vision* section of your blended learning blueprint and answer the following questions:

- What is your purpose? Why blended learning?
- How can you adapt existing blended learning models for your own context?
- What is the role of the teacher?
- What is the role of the student?

- What teaching practices are getting in the way of effective blended learning?

- How can you redesign the learning space to support blended learning?

Close your eyes for a moment. (Okay, first read the next few sentences and then close your eyes.) Envision your ideal learning space. Picture a school day that's going exactly the way you would like it to go. What are you doing? What are your students doing? Now open your eyes and look around. How close is that vision to your daily reality?

Thinking about vision is a good reminder that teaching is intentional; that is, blended learning is a means to achieve certain goals, aligned with purposes that are deeply aligned with what we believe about teaching and learning. Blended teaching is a deliberate use of instructional methods designed to increase equity, provide personalized learning opportunities, and empower students to control their own learning. I believe all educators (myself included) have room to become more intentional in our actions. With each instructional decision you make, know your *why*.

> Blended teaching is a deliberate use of instructional methods designed to increase equity, provide personalized learning opportunities, and empower students to control their own learning.

Knowing your *why* begins with an understanding of your own core values. When I work with teachers in professional learning settings, I often begin by asking teachers to clearly articulate their core values. This activity about our intentions usually goes something like this:

1. Develop a small list of core beliefs about student learning. First, brainstorm a long list of all of your core beliefs about teaching and learning. What do you believe to be true about teaching and learning (e.g., All students can learn; learning is social)?

2. Narrow your list to a smaller list (five or fewer) of core values. These essential truths guide the decisions you make as a teacher. Consider combining values into broader statements that encompass more than one idea.

3. Share your core values with a colleague you respect. Ask for feedback, and elaborate on why these values are important to you.

4. List instructional practices that are aligned with your core values. In other words, what are the choices you make and the strategies you use that allow you to carry out your beliefs? What is the evidence of your core values in your daily practice?

5. List instructional practices that are not aligned with your core values. Which instructional practices are in place just because that's how you've always done things? What practices oppose your core values?

Take time now to reflect on your core values and examine how blended learning can help you carry out those values. Perhaps return to Table 0.3 in the Introduction for specific examples of what blended learning looks like in the classroom to prompt your thinking. Use Table 2.1 to record your thoughts.

Now that you have taken the time to articulate what it is you believe to be true about teaching and learning, make these belief statements public. This might mean talking about them with your teammates, posting them in your classroom, or adding them to your email signature. Sharing our beliefs publicly can help us hold ourselves accountable to prioritizing the things that really matter and help others (students, colleagues, administrators) understand why we do what we do. In this chapter, we'll explore how a new vision for teaching and learning can help you carry out your core values.

Adapting Blended Models

As I mentioned in the Introduction, blended learning models can be helpful in casting a new vision for teaching and learning, but only to a certain extent. Exploring ways that agreed-upon models are enacted in diverse classrooms can be particularly helpful because you will find that any given model can have countless iterations in various settings. Ultimately, selecting a blended learning model depends on several factors, including school scheduling constraints, district policies, and availability of digital content and devices. Keep

Table 2.1 Core Values and Blended Learning

What are your core values?	How can blended learning help you enact your core values?

in mind that the blended learning models identified in the Introduction can be adapted and even merged to design a model that works best for you and your students.

Despite the limitations of this model-centric way of thinking, choosing a model or structure for blended learning in your classroom is a good starting place for your transition to blended learning. Following are a few strategies that could serve as catalysts for crafting a vision for blended learning in your classroom:

- Visit a colleague's classroom. Take note of the teacher's role and the students' role. Consider how the teacher uses time and space to his or her advantage. Observe procedures and routines that assist with managing the blended environment. (Looking for a school to visit? Take a look at pl.cmslearns.org to read about the personalized learning initiative in Charlotte-Mecklenburg Schools. Contact them to schedule a visit to a blended elementary school.)

- Read *Blended: Using Disruptive Innovation to Improve Schools,* by Michael B. Horn and Heather Staker (2014), to dive deeper into models of blended learning.

- Visit www.christenseninstitute.org to explore articles, videos, and case studies of blended learning.

- Visit betterlesson.com to hear from master blended teachers and see videos of blended learning in action.

Resource Spotlight

One of the most powerful tools I have found for assisting teachers in the shift toward a new vision for teaching and learning is BetterLesson's Blended Master Teacher Project, a free resource dedicated to "making effective blended learning practice visible and accessible to every educator around the world" (http://betterlesson.com/blended_learning). The Master Teacher Project provides videos and other artifacts from eleven blended teachers who were identified as master blended teachers after a rigorous selection process. The most helpful resource in this project for changing mindsets is a video reflection from each of the eleven blended master teachers describing their mindsets. Listening to these master teachers describe their mindsets can help teachers and administrators consider a new vision for teaching and learning. At betterlesson.com, you can also learn more about how teachers adapt blended learning models for their own unique contexts.

Rethinking the Role of Teachers and Learners

To truly live up to the definition of blended learning in our classrooms, in which students have control over time, place, path, and/or pace through an integrated learning experience, it goes without saying that the role of the teacher needs to be reexamined. The traditional view of the teacher's role—as the person responsible for knowing all the answers, for designing and delivering whole-group lessons, for controlling the pace of learning—will not help us carry out a new vision for teaching and learning.

Earlier in this chapter, when you closed your eyes to envision your ideal classroom, what did you see yourself doing? Were you at the front of the room talking to a classroom full of students? Teaching a small-group reading lesson? Meeting individually with a student for a writing conference? Were you sitting at a desk, watching a student presentation? Were you designing online content? Giving thoughtful, personalized feedback?

And what did you envision your students doing? Were they sitting at desks, facing the front of the room, eagerly waiting for words of wisdom to flow from your tongue? Frantically taking notes? Filling in bubbles on an answer sheet? Were they outside, making scientific observations and asking questions? On the floor in a corner of the room, brainstorming solutions to a problem? Presenting findings from a student-led research project? Working through digital content with a partner?

In a blended elementary classroom, you might observe any of these teacher and student roles at any time. The key is that these roles are *flexible*. And focused on what the *student needs* rather than what the *teacher wants*.

Ouch.

I know that can be a difficult pill to swallow. Trust me, I sometimes think first about what works best for me and second about what would work best for my students. There's only so much time in the day, and sometimes it may be easier and faster to plan a whole-group lesson than to plan for multiple small-group lessons. But if we want to shift away from teacher-centered toward student-led practices, we must begin with a different perspective on student and teacher roles. Blended learning gives us the structure, the time, and the tools to make that happen—to reimagine what it means to be an elementary teacher. Consider the teacher and student roles in a blended elementary classroom listed in Table 2.2. How are these roles similar to and different from the current reality in your classroom?

Tables 2.3 and 2.4 show two brief lesson plans with the same learning objective but very different roles for the teacher and students. Examine each lesson plan with an eye toward choice, control, and pacing. As educator and author Alan November asks, who owns the learning?

Table 2.2 Teacher and Student Roles in a Blended Elementary Classroom

Teacher Role	Student Role
The teacher creates learning experiences that are aligned with learning outcomes and based on student needs and interests.	The student selects tasks based on learning needs, interests, and learning modality preferences.
The teacher observes student work and confers individually with students to meet needs that arise.	The student completes tasks at his or her own pace, using digital and physical resources.
The teacher provides targeted small-group instruction based on observations, student work, and data from formative assessments.	The student completes formative assessments to check progress toward learning outcomes.
The teacher provides personalized feedback to help each student progress toward learning outcomes.	The student records and tracks data and feedback to assist with making future learning decisions.
The teacher provides the next pathway for students when they are ready.	The student moves on to the next pathway, at his or her own pace, after demonstrating mastery of learning outcomes.

Table 2.3 Lesson Plan in a Nonblended Elementary Classroom

Learning Objective	3.NF.A.3 [Common Core Math, Third-Grade, Numbers and Fractions Standard A] Explain equivalence of fractions in special cases, and compare fractions by reasoning about their size. Students will identify equivalent fractions.
Assessment	Students will complete a fractions quiz at the end of the week.
Instructional Sequence	The teacher will define *equivalent* and write a few examples of equivalent numbers on the board using what students already know about place value. 4 tens is equivalent to 40 350 is equivalent to 3 hundreds and 5 tens 8 tens is equivalent to 80 ones The teacher will use base ten blocks to model how these numbers are equivalent. The teacher will explain that fractions can be equivalent even if they don't look the same. Using fraction circles, the teacher will demonstrate examples of equivalent fractions, writing the equivalent fractions next to each model. Students will use individual fraction circle sets and a worksheet to practice identifying equivalent fractions. The teacher will move through the classroom and help students as they complete the worksheet. At the end of the lesson, the teacher explains that students will complete the back side of the worksheet for homework.

Letting Go of Control

According to the Christensen definition, a blended learning classroom allows students to have some control over time, place, path, and pace. To transfer control to learners, a critical shift must take place in a blended classroom: a shift from teacher-centered instruction to student-led learning. True blended

Table 2.4 Lesson Plan in a Blended Elementary Classroom

Learning Objective	3.NF.A.3 Explain equivalence of fractions in special cases, and compare fractions by reasoning about their size. Students will identify equivalent fractions.
Assessment	Students will respond to a four-question pre-assessment about equivalent fractions using Plickers cards. The teacher will use pre-assessment results to divide students into small groups for the lesson. Following the lesson, the teacher will ask the same four questions as a post-assessment for students who missed one or more questions on the pre-assessment. The teacher will use Plickers for the post-assessment. Students will record today's pre- and post-assessment data in their data notebooks.
Instructional Sequence	Students who answer all four pre-assessment questions correctly will watch a teacher-created video about comparing fractions with unlike denominators and work in pairs using fraction circles to complete a comparing fractions activity.
	Students who missed one or two questions on the pre-assessment will complete an EDpuzzle lesson that includes a teacher-created video demonstration identifying equivalent fractions. The lesson will ask students to use fraction circles and fraction strips to identify equivalent fractions. Students will receive immediate feedback on the questions they answer.
	Students who missed three or four questions on the pre-assessment will work in a small group with the teacher to practice identifying equivalent fractions using a variety of manipulatives, including fraction circles, pattern blocks, fraction strips, and Unifix cubes.

learning requires teachers to let go of control, but blended learning actually provides an avenue to help teachers to make this transition (see Figure 2.1).

Let's take a moment to clarify practices that are teacher-centered, student-centered, and student-led. In a teacher-centered classroom, the teacher controls the learning experience. The teacher is the primary source of content, and all instruction is driven from teacher-selected and teacher-paced assignments and lessons. Instruction in a teacher-centered classroom primarily takes place in a whole-group setting, with the teacher doing most of the talking.

A student-centered classroom is still driven by the teacher but allows for more student choice. Students may complete different tasks or access different types of content, but the teacher drives the structure of choice. The teacher may assign students to different learning stations or groups based on data or preference, or students may make choices within a specified list

Figure 2.1 Shift Toward Student-Led Instruction

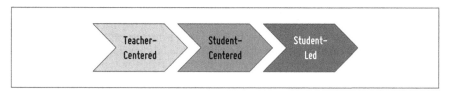

of tasks. Assessment data are tracked by the teacher and used to plan differentiated learning experiences. In a student-centered classroom, the teacher owns the learning experience but focuses on student needs in the process of planning and facilitating instruction.

Conversely, a student-led classroom is one in which students control the learning experience while the teacher serves as a facilitator, guide, and designer. Students work at their own paces, track their own data, set learning goals, and choose their own paths. In these classrooms, students have some level of control over when to engage in particular learning tasks (time), where learning occurs (place), which learning tasks to complete (path), and how long it takes to complete learning tasks (pace). The teacher designs a flexible learning environment, provides individualized coaching and feedback, and creates opportunities for students to engage in authentic learning experiences. In a student-led classroom, students control the pace of their own learning while the teacher guides students and offers instruction and feedback at the point of need.

In your transition to blended learning, take steps to move toward a more student-led classroom. This might mean beginning with a shift from teacher-centered to student-centered and later shifting from student-centered to student-led. The key is to make progress toward student-led learning to truly take advantage of what blended learning can offer. Examine the three lessons in Tables 2.5, 2.6, and 2.7 as examples of how you can shift from teacher-centered toward student-led. On the left, you will find a primarily teacher- or student-centered lesson. On the right, you will see how this lesson could be adapted to be more student-centered or student-led. In the student-led section, look for evidence of student control over time, place, path, or pace.

Table 2.5 Third-Grade Math Teacher-Centered and Student-Centered Lessons

Teacher-Centered Lesson	Student-Centered Lesson
The teacher begins by writing a 2-digit by 1-digit multiplication problem on the board. The teacher explains that today's lesson will present three strategies for solving 2-digit by 1-digit multiplication problems.	The teacher begins by writing a 2-digit by 1-digit multiplication problem on the board and asking if anyone knows how to solve it. The teacher calls on students who raise their hands and allows three different students to come to the board to solve the problem.
The teacher lists three strategies for solving multiplication problems and demonstrates how to use each strategy to solve the problem on the board. Students take notes in their math notebooks.	The teacher points out that the students used two different strategies to solve the problem. The teacher writes the names of those strategies on the board and adds a third strategy to the list. The teacher distributes copies of a diagram showing how to use each strategy and models how to use each strategy to solve a new 2-digit by 1-digit multiplication problem on the board.

Teacher-Centered Lesson	Student-Centered Lesson
The teacher distributes a worksheet containing fifteen 2-digit by 1-digit multiplication problems. The teacher works out the first problem on the board while students follow along. The teacher then assigns the remaining problems to the students and asks students to solve them quietly.	The teacher explains that students will work in three stations to practice using the three strategies. At each station, students will work collaboratively to apply a different strategy to a set of 2-digit by 1-digit multiplication problems. If students finish solving all problems at a station, they can play a partner math game before rotating to the next station.
After fifteen minutes, the teacher collects the worksheets and announces that students who did not finish all fifteen problems must complete the worksheet for homework.	As students rotate through stations, the teacher calls five students to her small-group table for guided practice applying the three strategies. These students were identified based on a diagnostic math assessment given the week before this lesson.

Table 2.6 First-Grade Literacy Student-Centered and Student-Led Lessons

Student-Centered Lesson	Student-Led Lesson
The teacher calls all students to the whole-class meeting area and teaches a seven-minute whole-class mini-lesson about reading with fluency. The teacher models what it sounds like to read fluently.	The teacher asks students to take out their data notebooks and find their fluency data tracker. Students review their data from recent fluency assessments. Students meet with their accountability partners to set and share this week's goals for fluency.
The teacher explains today's reading station tasks related to fluency. All students rotate through five stations, spending ten minutes at each station. Stations involve timed fluency practice with a partner, listening to a read aloud online, a sight word game, and other fluency tasks.	Students select from a variety of fluency tasks to help them work toward their fluency goals. Tasks involve timed fluency practice with a partner, listening to a read aloud online, a sight word game, and other fluency tasks. Students work at their own paces, moving on to a new task when ready or repeating the same task as often as needed.
As students work, the teacher calls students one at a time to complete an individual fluency assessment. He uses these assessment data to plan fluency stations for the next day.	As students work, the teacher calls students one at a time to complete an individual fluency assessment. Students add data from this assessment to their fluency data tracker and discuss progress toward their fluency goals with the teacher. The teacher asks students how the tasks they're working on today are helping them meet their goals.

Table 2.7 Fifth-Grade Science Student-Centered and Student-Led Lessons

Student-Centered Lesson	Student-Led Lesson
The teacher shows a short video from a local meteorologist explaining how meteorologists use technology to do their jobs. As students watch the video, they fill in answers to guiding questions provided by the teacher.	The teacher reads aloud the driving question for the current project-based learning (PBL) unit: *What if the weather never changed?* The teacher asks students to get into their PBL groups and quickly review their status on the project and discuss their goals for today.

(Continued)

Table 2.7 (Continued)

Student–Centered Lesson	Student–Led Lesson
Students work on a weather choice board, selecting tasks related to the unit's learning objectives. All students must complete three tasks by the end of the week. Choice board tasks include tracking weather over time, using forecast simulators, reading about weather systems, and watching videos about climate change. As they work, the teacher answers students' questions and provides resources as needed.	Students work in their PBL groups to answer the driving question. One group analyzes weather data they have tracked over the last several weeks. A different group reads and discusses an article about current droughts and floods in the United States. Another group watches a video about climate change. As they work, the teacher checks in with each group and provides guidance as needed.
The teacher provides students with a new set of questions about weather patterns and explains that students will use their time in the computer lab later today to search for answers.	After today's work time, the teacher asks each group about the final product they are planning to create to share their answers to the driving question. One group plans to record a weather video. Another group plans to write a scientific report. A different group plans to create a detailed weather map.

To make the shift toward student-led learning, the teacher must be willing to let go of certain practices. These practices will hinder your ability to design and facilitate blended and personalized learning. Table 2.8 identifies some practices to let go and suggests alternate practices to consider.

Transferring control to learners is not something that can happen overnight. To help students own their learning, we must deliberately teach certain ways of thinking and being in the classroom, many of which will be very different from students' past schooling experiences. Consider the following practices that need to be explicitly taught, modeled, and practiced to help students take on more ownership of their learning:

- How to analyze assessment data

- How to set goals that are measurable and attainable

- How to make appropriate choices about learning tasks

- When to abandon a task

- When and how to ask for help from the teacher

- Where and how to access content, tasks, and resources

Determine which of these practices your students need the most support with, and plan mini-lessons and guided practice opportunities, just as you would if you were teaching a new content-specific concept or process. In the blended elementary classroom, it is extremely important not to overlook the processes and procedures needed to help students manage their own learning experience.

> Transferring control to learners is not something that can happen overnight.

Table 2.8 Letting Go of Control

Practices to Let Go	Alternate Practices for the Blended Classroom
Stop delivering content in one way and assigning the same tasks for all students. One-size-fits-all does not work.	Start facilitating digital learning experiences that lead to personalized pathways for students.
Stop being the sole source of content and assigning tasks that are disconnected from an authentic, relevant purpose.	Start using student-centered instructional strategies that are connected to real-world applications.
Stop asking all students to process content, interact with others, and show what they know in the same way.	Start providing opportunities for students to make choices about content, process, and product.
Stop waiting until the end of a chunk of instruction to find out how students are progressing toward learning outcomes.	Start using frequent digital formative assessments for immediate feedback on student learning.
Stop talking to the whole class and using rigid student grouping structures.	Start implementing flexible student configurations, focusing on individual and small-group instruction with minimal whole-group instruction.
Stop planning instruction days in advance with no room for flexibility based on student progress and response to instruction.	Start being responsive to student progress, making immediate adjustments based on data and feedback.

FOR THE LOW-TECH CLASSROOM

You don't need to have a device for every student to carry out a new vision for teaching and learning. The beauty of blended learning is that it gives the teacher flexibility to use any combination of digital and nondigital learning experiences. If you and your students have limited access to technology, you will want to select a blended learning model that does not require multiple devices at a time. For example, you can initiate a station rotation model with only one technology-based station and a few hands-on collaborative or independent stations. Additionally, the lab rotation model does not require any devices within the classroom, relying instead on a stationary or mobile technology lab. The key is to find a way to transfer control of the learning experience from yourself to your students, which relies more on changing your mindset than on purchasing devices.

DonorsChoose matches teachers with potential donors to help fund classroom projects. If you are transitioning to blended and personalized learning, you can use that as a rationale to justify your need for devices. Be sure to visit donorschoose.org and consider posting your own project.

Redesigning the Learning Space

As we'll explore in the next chapter, blended learning allows the teacher to think differently about how best to use time during the school day. Similarly, a transition to blended learning provides an opportunity for the elementary teacher to reconsider how best to use space in the learning environment.

The typical elementary classroom tends to be a fairly flexible environment. However, to implement blended learning, shift the roles of teacher and student, and move to a student-led learning environment, we need to rethink how we structure and make use of space and resources. Master blended teachers have learned to think more flexibly about the space in and around their classrooms and leverage a variety of resources that are available. Designing a space that allows students to make choices, provides room for both independent and collaborative work, and fosters small-group and one-on-one instruction requires intention and creativity.

One of the first considerations in redesigning the learning space is the model you've selected or adapted to guide your transition to blended learning. The specific model(s) you included in your vision statement will guide how you shape the learning environment. If a station rotation model works best for you and your students, then you'll need to design multiple spaces for small groups to interact with content and one another. If you're transitioning to a flipped classroom, you will need to create large, open spaces that are flexible enough for a variety of whole-class, small-group, and individual exploration and interaction. See photos from flexible classrooms in Figures 2.2, 2.3, and 2.4.

Figure 2.2 Charlotte-Mecklenburg Schools' Grand Oak Elementary School includes a variety of comfortable working spaces for students

Figure 2.3 Flexible seating and organized materials allow students to choose how to use the space

Figure 2.4 Grand Oak Elementary School has teacher-designed zones for different types of learning

In your transition to blended learning, consider how you can minimize whole-group spaces and maximize room for individuals and small groups to work together. Ask your students for input in designing a flexible and inviting learning space. Visit other classrooms and schools for ideas. And don't forget about Pinterest as a place for classroom redesign inspiration. Most blended elementary classrooms will share many of the same types of spaces, such as those listed in Table 2.9.

Other considerations to keep in mind in your redesign are noise level and flow. In a blended elementary classroom, some students may be engaged in collaborative problem solving while others are writing about self-selected topics or working through an adaptive software program. At the same time, the teacher may be meeting individually with students to provide feedback on their most recent learning goals. To allow these diverse types of experiences to occur simultaneously, the environment must first be designed to accommodate each learner and each type of task.

Consider creating different noise "zones" in your classroom to accommodate students who need a quieter space without limiting collaborative work. Also, take some time to map out ways movement in the classroom should flow to help students be thoughtful of other learners and avoid walking past twelve different students on the way to get a Chromebook from the cart. Appropriate noise level and flow can be taught and practiced through short mini-lessons and role play at the beginning of the year and revisited as needed to remind students of expectations for managing the learning environment.

Table 2.9   Spaces and Resources in a Flexible Blended Learning Classroom

Learning Space	Uses	Resources to Have Available
Small-Group Table	Targeted small-group instruction, collaborative projects, peer feedback, work station	Devices, individual whiteboards and markers or a whiteboard table top, writing utensils, sticky notes
Space for Quiet, Independent Work	Independent reading or writing, online work, individual conferencing, partner reading	Comfortable seating (bean bags, stools, rugs, exercise balls, folding chairs), desks, short tables
Presentation Station	Mini-lessons, student presentations, read alouds, shared reading or writing	Director's chair, tall stool, rocking chair, document camera, projector, whiteboard or easel, pocket chart
Rolling Cart	Mobile work station, impromptu small-group instruction, makerspace	Individual whiteboards and markers, craft supplies, games, books, clipboards, writing utensils
Charging Station	Store and charge devices	Cart, shelves, dividers, charging cords, access to power outlet

In a blended elementary classroom, another learning space that requires thoughtful design is the online learning environment. Online content should be accessible to all learners and organized logically. With elementary learners in particular, online content navigation should be simple and consistent. If you use a learning management system (LMS) such as Canvas, Blackboard, or Schoology, use a consistent format (I prefer modules) so that content is always organized in the same way. Consider using consistent signposts or icons to indicate specific types of content, and use images and video to provide multiple opportunities for interacting with content. Additional tips for online design are provided in the following box.

Tips for Online Content Design

- Break content into meaningful chunks.

- Use a clean, simple structure that limits distractions.

- Use buttons on your home page to quickly link students to the most important content.

- Embed web content into your LMS to avoid sending students to multiple sites.

- Use a tool such as Symbaloo to visually organize bookmarks and allow students to quickly access frequently used sites.

- For younger students, limit text and use images and videos instead. (See samples of online content from a kindergarten classroom in Figures 2.5 and 2.6.)

- Use consistent formatting, organization, navigation, headings, and so forth. (See a sample content module from a fourth-grade classroom in Figure 2.7.)

(Continued)

(Continued)

Figure 2.5 Using symbols on a kindergarten Canvas page allows students to quickly find online activities

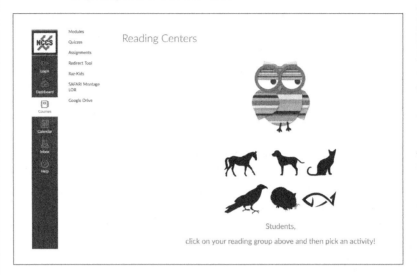

Source: Canvas, through Instructure. Content owned by NCCS.

Figure 2.6 Online lessons and resources for Mrs. Fitzgerald's reading groups are organized in a grid using Blendspace.com

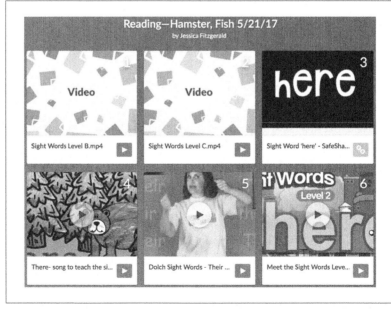

Source: Courtesy of Jessica Fitzgerald.

Figure 2.7 Fourth-grade teacher Melissa White organizes content and tasks into modules arranged by date and labeled with content standards to help students find what they need

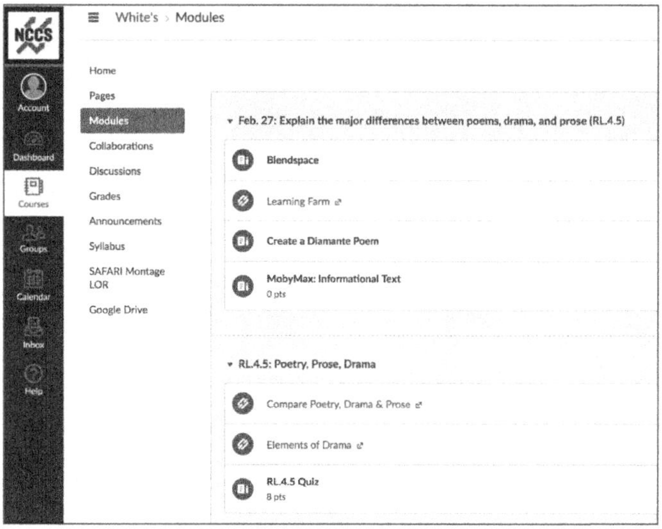

Source: Canvas, through Instructure. Content owned by NCCS.

Designing the Blueprint

Once new possibilities for teaching and learning have been identified and committed to, the real work of blended learning begins. Teachers, teams of teachers, schools, and districts must identify practices and processes that need to change to align the learning environment with the new vision. A vision without change will have no effect on student learning. As described in the Introduction, the benefits of blended learning are many, including equity, empowerment, and personalized learning for all students. However, we will never reap these benefits without a willingness to let go of teaching practices and educational processes that are standing in the way of a transformed learning environment.

Let's admit that we are creatures of habit. Change is hard. It's easier and more comfortable to maintain the status quo.

Let's also admit that our students deserve better.

Once you develop a new vision for teaching and learning that involves leveraging blended methods to meet each student's learning needs, the next step is to move forward and implement change. Complete the *Crafting Your Vision* section of the following blended learning blueprint to identify some starting places for change and improvement.

1. Crafting Your Vision

a. What is your purpose? Why blended learning?	b. How can you adapt existing blended learning models for your own context?

c. What is the role of the teacher?	d. What is the role of the student?

e. What teaching practices are getting in the way of effective blended learning?	f. How can you redesign the learning space to support blended learning?

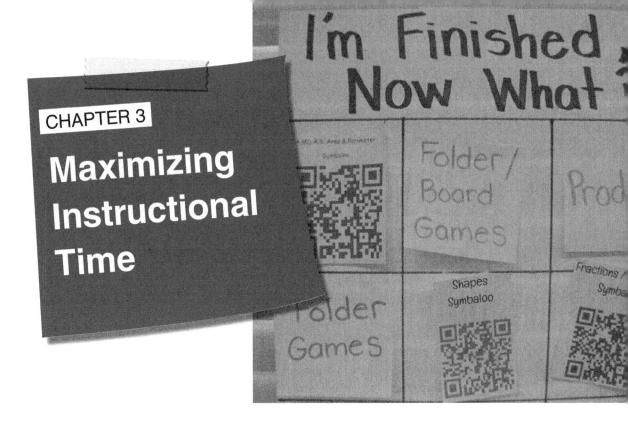

CHAPTER 3

Maximizing Instructional Time

In this chapter, we will consider the following strategies for maximizing time through blended learning:

- Answering the essential question about time

- Rethinking the school day

- Cloning the teacher

By the end of this chapter, you will be able to complete the *Maximizing Instructional Time* section of your blended learning blueprint and answer the following questions:

- What is the best way to use face-to-face instructional time?

- What is the best way to use digital learning opportunities?

- How can you rethink your daily and weekly schedule to leverage blended opportunities?

- How can you think about content in a more interconnected way?

- How can you "clone" yourself to provide multiple instances of targeted instruction?

- What are some missed opportunities resulting from how you use instructional time?

As I mentioned in the Introduction, blended learning leverages what's best about the face-to-face and online learning environments and allows teachers to think flexibly about how to make the best use of each. In this chapter, we will explore ideas for making the most of face-to-face and online learning in the blended elementary classroom and consider ways to maximize instructional time for all learners. Get ready to rethink how you structure time and use face-to-face and online opportunities.

Answering the Essential Question About Time

One of the first questions for teachers transitioning to a blended learning environment to consider is, What is the best use of face-to-face and online instruction? Regardless of how far along you are in the transition to a blended learning environment, you need to be able to answer this question with certainty. Your answer will be a major factor in how blended learning takes shape in your classroom.

Keep in mind that your answer to this question may be very different from someone else's. How you choose to leverage the affordances of the face-to-face environment and the online environment depends on factors that are specific to you, your students, and your context. To help you answer this essential question, consider the affordances and limitations of each setting listed in Table 3.1.

As I mentioned in the Introduction, blended elementary teachers let technology do what it's good at so they can do what they're good at. How can you leverage the affordances of the online learning environment to make more time for you to use your own strengths as a teacher? Use Table 3.2 to brainstorm which types of learning experiences in an elementary classroom would be best suited for the online environment and which would be best for the face-to-face environment. Include a brief rationale to support your thinking.

As we think about the use of time in a blended elementary classroom, keep in mind that not every student needs the same amount of time from us or the same amount of time to engage with a learning task. Many times, as teachers, we feel that we aren't being fair if some students get more of our time than others do or if some students are able to spend more time on tasks than others can. This type of thinking needs to be thrown out the window. In a blended classroom, each student gets the time and instruction she or he needs, regardless of how this compares with that of other students.

In most schools, all learners are given the same amount of time to meet the same learning outcomes. We know that students come to us with varying strengths, interests, background experiences, and prior knowledge, yet we continue to expect that all students should progress at the same pace. In

Table 3.1 Affordances and Limitations of Face-to-Face and Online Environments

	Face-to-Face	Online
Affordances	• Teacher provides just-in-time support and instruction • Students interact with teacher and peers in real time • Teacher uses nonverbal cues to gather information about students • Teacher uses real-world objects to help students learn • Students receive immediate feedback and redirection when needed • Teacher can adjust pace based on student progress	• Students engage with a variety of types of content • Adaptive software adjusts based on how students respond • Students receive immediate feedback • Students can have multiple attempts to master learning outcomes • Students work at their own paces • Teacher receives real-time data to make instructional decisions
Limitations	• Teacher can't always know what students are thinking or how they are progressing • Teacher-to-student ratio limits amount of individualized support available	• Teacher may not always be available when help is needed • Students may not possess the necessary technical skills • Students may choose content or tasks that just aren't right for them

these schools, time is constant, which means learning is a variable. Learning varies by student because not all students will learn at the same pace.

Rick DuFour, a professional learning communities (PLC) guru, argued that schools need to figure out a way to make time the variable so that learning is the constant (DuFour, DuFour, Eaker, & Many, 2006). If we vary how we use time to meet the specific needs of each student, we can expect that all students will learn. This fundamental shift in how we think about time and learning can lead to tremendous outcomes for our students, and luckily, a blended classroom provides a way for us to make this a reality, as depicted in Figures 3.1 and 3.2.

Rethinking the School Day

Blended environments provide an opportunity to rethink how we use and maximize instructional time. Imagine a typical literacy block in an elementary classroom. The teacher begins with a thirty-minute whole-group lesson focusing on a specific literacy skill or strategy. Students then rotate through stations, spending ten minutes at each station, with students completing the same tasks at each station. During these rotations, the teacher works with small groups, teaching the same literacy skill to each group. In some classrooms, students who do not complete station work within the allotted

Table 3.2 Leveraging Face-to-Face and Online Learning

Learning Experience	Face-to-Face or Online?	Rationale
Collaborative student projects		
Small-group instruction		
Formative assessments to determine progress		
Review of content that has not yet been mastered		
One-on-one conferences with students		
Introduction to a new topic of study		
Mini-lesson to teach a new procedure		
Literature-based discussion		
Working through the writing process		
Providing peer feedback		

Figure 3.1 In a blended kindergarten classroom, technology allows students to engage with tasks that adapt based on their responses and progress toward learning outcomes

time or to a satisfactory level are required to complete those tasks at lunch, during recess, or for homework.

Does this structure make the best use of the students' time? The teacher's time? Available resources? Let's consider each aspect of the literacy block described in the previous paragraph with an eye toward maximizing instructional time:

> A thirty-minute whole-group lesson most likely does not provide the instruction all students need at any given moment. For some students, the lesson may be just right and just-in-time. For others, the content or support structure of the lesson may not be the right fit or provided at the right time. A short, five- to seven-minute mini-lesson could be just as useful, freeing up more time for the teacher to meet student needs through individual or targeted small-group instruction.
>
> Rather than teaching the same small-group lesson to multiple groups over an hour or so, a more efficient use of time would be to teach a short whole-group mini-lesson followed by targeted small-group lessons or one-on-one conferences with students who need support. These small-group and individual opportunities should be tailored to specific student learning needs.
>
> In a blended classroom, students' work at stations is directed by students with guidance from the teacher. Students choose how to use their time,

Figure 3.2 Melissa White provides small-group math instruction while the rest of the class works on self-selected learning tasks

which resources to use, and how much time to spend on a task, and they are not punished for needing more time to master a concept, strategy, or skill. As I mentioned in the previous chapter, students need instruction and practice to take this level of ownership. However, this is a better use of time in the blended classroom than one-size-fits-all station work.

For an example of how to design a blended literacy block, look at the teacher plans in Figure 3.3. As you can see, the teacher uses time intentionally to meet the needs of individual learners and small groups. Further, notice that students are working on self-paced, adaptive tasks at stations.

One way to rethink the use of time and leverage the affordances of a blended environment is to design interdisciplinary learning experiences that challenge the notion of the school day as a collection of isolated, subject-specific chunks of time. Rather than planning separate blocks of time for literacy, math, and science instruction, consider the advantages of integrating content areas. A single project can incorporate learning outcomes from literacy, social studies, math, science, and the arts. Project-based learning (PBL) is a perfect fit for the blended elementary classroom, helping students make connections across content areas, explore issues that matter to them, leverage technology for research and public sharing, and direct their own learning. If you'd like to learn more about how to make PBL work

Figure 3.3 Teacher Plans for Elementary Literacy Block From Charlotte-Mecklenburg Schools

Small-Group/Tiered Assignments

- Teacher will assess each day through informal assessment to see how students are mastering.
- Groups can be larger or smaller based on how many rotation stations you want and how many students you have.

Groups	Students	Mini-Lesson	Station Rotation
1	Jack, Emma, Denzel, Juan, Thresa, Kathy	Adding and subtracting with fractions with like denominators	1. Collaboration* 2. Small group with me 3. Playlist/Pathway 4. DreamBox**/Khan
2	Nia, Donny Felipe, Katharine, Karissa, Dan	Adding and subtracting with fractions with unlike denominators	1. DreamBox 2. Playlist/Pathway 3. Small group with me 4. Collaboration
3	Genevie, Shawn, Torri, Josh Deandrea, Moses	Comparing/ordering fractions	1. Small group with me 2. Collaboration 3. DreamBox/Khan 4 Playlist/Pathway
4	Shaquita, Heather, Federico, Hannah, Teresa, Jeff	Multiplying and dividing fractions	1. Playlist/Pathway 2. DreamBox/Khan 3. Collaboration 4. Small group with me

* Collaboration is when students work together to do a H.O.T.S. [Higher Order Thinking Skills]. (Example: Creating a how-to video on adding and subtraction fractions, doing a math project, or games.)

** DreamBox adaptive learning platform that meets the students at their levels.

Conferencing Schedule

Notes on conferencing go in binder

	Group 1	Group 2	Group 3	Group 4
Monday	Jack, Emma	Nia, Donny	Genevie, Shawn	Shaquita, Heather
Tuesday	Denzel, Juan	Felipe, Katharine	Torri, Josh	Federico, Hannah
Wednesday	Thresa, Kathy	Karissa, Dan	Deandrea, Moses	Teresa, Jeff
Thursday	Based on needs or absents	Based on needs or absents	Based on needs or absents	Based on needs or absents
Friday	Based on needs or absents	Based on needs or absents.	Based on needs or absents.	Based on needs or absents

Source: Charlotte-Mecklenburg Schools Personalized Learning Department.

in an elementary classroom, I strongly recommend starting with *PBL in the Elementary Grades,* by Sara Hallermann, John Larmer, and John R. Mergendoller (2016).

We all know that the traditional school day can feel segmented and rushed, leaving little time for students to ask questions, explore new ideas, create a product of their learning, or get lost in a good book. We rush students along from one task to the next to "cover" the curriculum. Replacing this view with a more open perspective on structuring the school day can free up time for meaningful and lasting learning to take place. To make this happen, we must design uninterrupted chunks of time for students to engage deeply with content, interact meaningfully with each other, and reflect on their learning.

As you will see throughout this book, intentional time for student reflection and goal-setting is a nonnegotiable element of the blended elementary classroom. How else will students take ownership of their learning and make choices that are right for them? Deliberate, frequent reflection helps students identify the types of tasks that work best for them, monitor their progress toward learning outcomes, hold themselves accountable, and continue to refine their goals. Build time for reflection into the school day, and model this reflective practice yourself.

You are probably wondering how to make this work within the constraints of your school day or week. How can you best maximize the time available? Let's look at a sample schedule for a blended elementary classroom. Keep in mind that you must teach and practice routines and procedures to help students function effectively in a blended environment. We'll look closely at these routines and procedures in Chapter 4. For now, identify elements of the schedule in Table 3.3 that could help with your transition to blended learning and allow student control over time, place, path, and pace.

Notice how many opportunities students have for making choices, directing their own learning, and reflecting on their own progress. These pieces are essential as we implement blended learning and transition toward more student control of time, place, path, and pace. Also notice that there are very few times when the teacher talks to the whole class. Students lead much of the whole-group talk that takes place throughout the day, and most teacher-led instruction occurs in small groups or one-on-one.

Cloning the Teacher

One of my favorite things to talk about with blended teachers is the opportunity technology presents for them to clone themselves. Yes, you read that right. A blended classroom enables the teacher to clone herself. What

Table 3.3 Sample Daily Schedule for Blended Elementary Classroom

7:45 a.m.	*Students arrive* Students log into their weekly goal-setting and reflection template. Students reflect on what was accomplished the previous day to set goals for today.
8:15	*Classroom meeting* Student leader for the day facilitates a classroom meeting. In the meeting, students share their goals for the day and discuss any management issues that need to be addressed, such as respectful movement around the classroom, management of classroom resources, etc.
8:30	*Math pathway time* Students work on personalized pathways (more in Chapter 4) while the teacher facilitates targeted small-group math lessons. Students self-select from a variety of face-to-face and online learning tasks and work at their own paces. In between small-group lessons, the teacher checks in with a few students individually and provides support as needed. At the end of pathway time, students update their reflection and goal-setting templates and talk with their accountability partners about what they accomplished. With these partners, students share their goals for pathway time the following day.
10:00	*Brain break* Teacher uses GoNoodle (see Figure 3.4) to get students moving and help them focus for the next learning block.
10:15	*Literacy block* Teacher begins with a brief whole-class interactive reading experience. The teacher models and explicitly teaches effective comprehension strategies. Following shared reading, students self-select from a variety of literacy tasks, including independent reading, buddy reading, interactive literacy practice online, independent writing, peer editing, etc. Students choose where to work in the classroom and select which materials (digital or print) to use. The teacher facilitates targeted small-group reading and writing lessons based on each student's needs. Midway through the literacy block, students stop working and talk with their accountability partners about how they are using their time. Students set a goal for the remainder of the literacy block and return to work. The literacy block ends with all students updating their reflection and goal-setting templates and a few students publicly sharing what they learned or accomplished during the literacy block.
11:45	*Read aloud*
12:00 noon	*Lunch and recess*
1:15 p.m.	*Project-based learning* The student leader for the day provides a quick recap of where the class is with the current PBL unit and a reminder of expectations for the final product. One member from each PBL group provides a brief status report on what the group hopes to accomplish today. Students get into their PBL groups and continue working on their projects. The teacher floats around the room to assist groups as needed. Students use a variety of resources to research, write, and create. At the end of this time, groups reflect on what they accomplished and determine their next steps.
2:30	*Reflection and goal-setting* Students update their reflection and goal-setting templates, reflecting on how well they met the goals they set that morning. Students talk with their accountability partners before leaving for the day.
2:45	*Dismissal*

Figure 3.4   Kindergarten students in Jessica Fitzgerald's classroom use GoNoodle regularly for brain breaks

Source: Courtesy of Jessica Fitzgerald. GoNoodle, Inc. gonoodle.com

> A blended classroom enables the teacher to clone herself.

I mean is that the teacher can be in more than one place at the same time, providing targeted support to multiple students or groups of students at once. Examine Figure 3.5, which depicts a blended elementary classroom where the teacher leverages technology to clone herself throughout the classroom.

In this particular classroom, students in four different groups are participating in targeted, teacher-created learning experiences. Each group is receiving tailored instruction with the ability for both teacher and students to receive immediate, real-time feedback on their work. This teacher is maximizing instructional time by essentially being in four places at once. While the teacher facilitates a small-group lesson, he can also monitor his teacher dashboard on the web tools students are using to track their progress in real time. As students respond to questions in Nearpod, for example, the teacher can immediately determine which students completed the task proficiently and which need more support. Rather than waiting until the end of the literacy block, the teacher is able to identify immediately who needs support and determine how best to provide that support. As soon as the current small-group lesson is finished, the teacher can pull a new small group based on real-time data from the cloned lessons.

Figure 3.5 Cloning the Teacher in a Blended Elementary Classroom

Multiple types of instruction can be cloned and shared with students. Following is a list of possible learning experiences to clone:

- Demonstrate a process, such as how to navigate a website, how to conduct a peer review, how to submit an assignment, or how to read like a writer.

- Record a mini-lesson so that students can watch it as often as needed.

- Record a read aloud, embedding opportunities for students to stop and apply comprehension strategies to the text.

- Model a think aloud, making visible learning strategies with a variety of types of content.

- Record instructions for a complex task, allowing students to pause and replay as often as needed.

- Provide an example or non-example of a completed product.

CLASSROOM MANAGEMENT IN THE BLENDED CLASSROOM

For these cloning strategies to be effective, students must be able to work for extended periods without the teacher, who needs to give his or her attention to a specific group of students. Know that this may not happen on day one or day nine or probably even day twenty-five. To help students develop independence, try the following strategies:

- Use a visual symbol to remind students not to interrupt your lesson. This could be a stop sign at your small-group table or a particular hat or lanyard you wear during small-group lessons.

- As a class, set a goal for how long students should be able to work independently or in stations. Use a timer to record how long students stay focused and on task, and track the class's progress visually. Celebrate when you reach your goal, and then set a new goal. Continue building stamina bit by bit.

- Implement the "ask three before me" rule to avoid being bombarded with questions. With this rule, a student who has a question must ask three other people in the classroom before coming to you.

In the next chapter, we will look closely at specific procedures and routines that must be established to make the blended classroom work.

Table 3.4 lists a few of my favorite tools for cloning the teacher. Consider how you might organize and store these lessons for students to access quickly and easily when needed. You might use your school's learning management system (LMS), or you might use a social bookmarking platform such as Diigo, tagging each resource with a keyword.

Once you have taken the time to clone yourself using some of the tools listed in this chapter, you can take advantage of these teacher-created materials by sharing them with your teammates. Imagine a team of teachers, each designing interactive learning experiences with embedded assessments and feedback opportunities, sharing these lessons with one another to increase the impact on student learning. This collaboration eases the workload on each teacher and provides a unique opportunity for students to learn from multiple educators with different strengths, styles, and strategies. Over time, you and your colleagues can build a database of teacher-created content and learning experiences and

> Over time, you and your colleagues can build a database of teacher-created content and learning experiences and allow students to access what they need when they need it as often as they need it.

Table 3.4   Tools and Processes for Cloning the Teacher

Tools	Clone the Teacher
Screencasting tools (Screencast-O-Matic, Screencastify, Snagit, Educreations)	Create a recording of what's on your screen along with your webcam to allow students to see and hear you while you demonstrate or model a process. Screencast-O-Matic is free and works on any computer. Screencastify works only in Chrome. Snagit is a paid subscription software for creating screenshots and screencasts. Use the Educreations app to record screencasts from your mobile device. See an example of a screencast in Figure 3.6.
Nearpod	Create an interactive slide show (or upload an existing slide deck) and embed formative assessments, such as multiple-choice, open-ended, and drawn-response items. To clone yourself, consider combining screencasting with Nearpod for an even more powerful learning experience. First, record a screencast demonstrating a process, reading a text, or teaching a mini-lesson. Next, upload your video to Nearpod. Add some content slides if needed. Finally, add question slides to ask students to apply what they learned from the screencast. (See Figure 3.7.)
PlayPosit and EDpuzzle	PlayPosit and EDpuzzle allow you to embed questions throughout a video, turning a passive experience into an interactive one and providing you with real-time feedback about student learning. Again, consider creating a mash-up using screencasting and either PlayPosit or EDpuzzle to embed questions into your screencast, as shown in Figure 3.8.

Figure 3.6   Use a screencasting tool to demonstrate a complex task or record a mini-lesson

Source: EDU 654 Literature Review Blog. Published by Jayme Linton.

Figure 3.7 In Nearpod, real-time responses from students are visible to the teacher

Source: Nearpod, nearpod.com

Figure 3.8 PlayPosit allows teachers to embed questions or discussion prompts throughout a video, requiring students to pause the video and respond

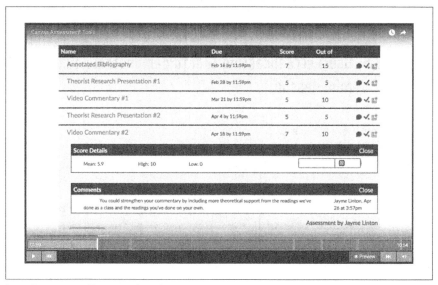

Source: Photo courtesy of http://www.playposit.com

FOR THE LOW-TECH CLASSROOM

If you and your students have limited access to devices, you can still leverage technology to clone yourself. At each station, you might only have one device that all students at that station share. For example, if you have recorded a screencast demonstrating how to simplify fractions, all students at one station can gather around a shared device to watch the lesson. Afterward, each student in that station might work through a few simplifying fraction problems with fraction rods and whiteboards. With one device at each cloned station, a few devices can go a long way.

allow students to access what they need when they need it as often as they need it.

Designing the Blueprint

It's now time to think about how you can put these strategies to work to maximize instructional time. You may want to start small, trying out just one of these changes at a time. Perhaps you're ready to think about ways to clone yourself to provide targeted instruction to multiple individuals or groups at once. Or maybe it's time to rethink how you schedule the school day to make better use of your time and your students' time. Or you may need to rethink the types of learning experiences you plan for the face-to-face environment and the online environment. Complete the *Maximizing Instructional Time* section of the blended learning blueprint to identify possibilities and starting points for your blended classroom.

2. Maximizing Instructional Time

a. What is the best way to use face-to-face instructional time?	b. What is the best way to use digital learning opportunities?

c. How can you rethink your daily/weekly schedule to leverage blended opportunities?	d. How can you think about content in a more interconnected way?

e. How can you "clone" yourself to provide multiple instances of targeted instruction?	f. What are some missed opportunities resulting from how you use instructional time?

CHAPTER 4

Making It Personal

In this chapter, we will consider the following elements of personalized learning:

- Moving from differentiation to personalized learning

- Designing personalized pathways

- Making pathways work

By the end of this chapter, you will be able to complete the *Making It Personal* section of your blended learning blueprint and answer the following questions:

- How can you move from differentiated instruction toward personalized learning?

- How might you structure personalized pathways?

- How can you give students control over time, place, path, and pace?

- What routines and procedures do you need to establish, teach, and practice?

- What will be the teacher's role as students work on pathway tasks?

- What challenges do you anticipate? How might you solve them?

In Chapter 2, we analyzed components of a new vision for the blended elementary classroom. In Chapter 3, we examined ways to maximize instructional time and use technology to our advantage. In this chapter, we will explore strategies and processes for using blended methods to shift to personalized learning.

Shifting from a classroom that is largely teacher-directed toward one that is flexible and personalized can be a difficult transition for any teacher. This shift, however, is at the crux of blended learning. As I mentioned previously, blended learning enables teachers to be more responsive to student needs. Successful blended teachers leverage technology to use real-time data, observation, and interaction with students to design personalized learning experiences. Let's explore what personalized learning can look like in the blended elementary classroom.

Moving From Differentiation to Personalized Learning

I hope, as you read this book, you are continuously designing and redesigning your vision for teaching and learning in your classroom as you consider ways to help students take control of their learning. Blended learning simply provides the structure and tools that enable us to rethink the role of the teacher and student and to enact this new vision. As I mentioned in the Introduction, implementing blended learning is not the goal. We are looking for ways to help our students reach important academic, social, and personal goals. Blended learning is a method that helps us do that. It's a means to a very important end.

A teacher can use a blended learning model to enact nearly any philosophy or vision of teaching and learning. In an elementary classroom, blended learning could be used to perpetuate a traditional teacher-centered approach, with technology serving only as a tool for students to complete one-size-fits-all assignments. Or, blended learning can provide a means by which all students are given the time and support they need and are empowered to take ownership of their learning. My goal in this book is to help you leverage blended methods to increase equity and meet your learners' needs through personalized learning.

Think back to the core values you identified in Chapter 2, and consider how blended learning can help you carry out those values in your classroom. Figure 4.1 illustrates how blended learning can be used to enact

Figure 4.1 Differentiation, Individualized Learning, or Personalized Learning in a Blended Classroom

Philosophy	Teacher Role	Student Role	Illustrative Examples
Differentiation	The teacher owns and controls the learning experience based on assessment data. Teacher uses whole-group instruction but tailors practice based on different levels of student needs and preferences.	The student meets the requirements given to them based on their needs.	• Literature circles around different texts but same theme • Grouping students based on levels but delivering same content • Tic-tac-toe board
Individualized Learning	The teacher drives instruction through teacher-created lessons, tasks, and projects.	Student and teacher own the learning experience. The student has choice in tasks and/or products.	• Teacher paces out the curriculum • Choice boards or playlists • Dreambox or Compass Learning (adaptive programs)
Personalized Learning	The teacher facilitates learning through student questioning, conferencing, and providing feedback. No whole-group instruction but small-group direct instruction based on needs. They are organizers of learning opportunities.	The student owns the learning experience through pace, complex problems, and choice. They actively pursue new knowledge and consistently self-evaluate, self-regulate, and self-motivate.	• Students work at their own pace using pathways • Student-led conferences • Student achieves mastery based on demonstrated ability and performance
Blended Learning	Student owns the learning experience, by control over the time, place, playlists, and/or pace. Teacher and/or student generates task design based on identified software platform or series or learning experiences. *Blended Learning is a delivery system connected to one of the philosophies.*		

various philosophies of teaching. In this chapter, we'll look closely at how we can use blended learning as a conduit for personalized learning in our classrooms.

To examine how we might transition from a differentiated to a personalized environment, let's use a common instructional approach used in many elementary classrooms: work stations (see Figures 4.2 and 4.3).

Elementary teachers have been using a station approach for years, including literacy stations, math centers, and more recently science, technology, engineering, arts, and math (STEAM) stations. Some teachers may assume that simply using a station model implies alignment with a blended

Figure 4.2 An "I can" statement provides direction for students working at an engineering station

Figure 4.3 Science and literacy are integrated through STEAM (science, technology, engineering, arts, and math) stations in Caitlan Reese's fifth-grade classroom

learning approach. This isn't necessarily the case, however. Let's look at how teachers could use a station approach to perpetuate either a teacher-centered, differentiated, or personalized learning environment (Table 4.1). Later in this chapter and the next, we will explore ways to support students in transitioning toward taking more ownership of the learning experience.

Consider which of these types of practices is more common in your classroom. If most of your instructional practices tend to be more teacher-centered, you may need to identify areas where you can give up some control of the learning experience and help students take ownership of their learning. In my experience, teacher control is often the thing that gets in the way of a new vision for teaching and learning. Examine the shifts that should take place as teachers move from differentiated to personalized (see Table 4.2).

Table 4.1 Using Stations for Teacher-Centered, Differentiated, and Personalized Learning

Teacher-Centered	Differentiated	Personalized
• The teacher designs learning tasks for each station. • All students move through the same stations at the same pace. • All students complete the same task(s) at each station. • Student groupings for stations are rigid and inflexible.	• The teacher designs learning tasks for each station. • All students move through the same stations at the same pace. • Students may choose which tasks to complete or work on tasks that have been differentiated by the teacher according to student need. • The teacher meets with small groups for targeted instruction. • Student groups for stations are flexible and fluid.	• The teacher designs stations that include a variety of ways for students to engage with content. • Students self-select stations and tasks based on their own learning needs. • Students spend different amounts of time at stations depending on need and interest. • Students reflect on their progress and set goals. • The teacher meets with small groups for targeted instruction. • The teacher coaches students one-on-one and provides individualized feedback.

Table 4.2 Instructional Shifts in a Personalized Classroom

Shift away from . . .	Toward . . .
The teacher as sole provider of content	Students interact with and create digital content
One-size-fits-all instruction	Personalized pathways for students
Teacher-paced instruction	Student control over time and pace
Teacher ownership of student assessment data	Student ownership of data for driving their own learning
Whole-group instruction	Targeted instruction through small groups and individual conferences
Grades to communicate student progress	Immediate feedback aligned with learning outcomes

To move toward personalized learning, there must be time for the teacher and students to learn more about how students learn best. Many blended elementary classrooms utilize learner profiles to help students think about their interests and strengths, reflect on how they learn best, and choose tasks that are a good fit for them. These profiles also help the teacher design tasks that will be interesting and engaging for students. A learner profile can be as simple as a piece of paper or as complex as a digital program that adjusts as students update their preferences. Google Forms is a great tool for designing a learner profile. With Google Forms, you can easily make changes to the learner profile and quickly access student responses. See an example in Figure 4.4. A learner profile for younger students might include pictures instead of or along with text. Have students update their learner profiles at various points throughout the school year as their interests and strengths change.

A learner profile is a great starting place for a shift toward personalized learning in a blended classroom. Making students and teachers aware of the optimal conditions for learning for each child can help teachers and students make better choices in designing and selecting learning tasks. Keep in mind that the learner profile is constantly changing as the learner continues to grow and develop new interests along with new areas of strength and opportunities for growth. Revisit students' learning profiles as a regular part of your work with students in stations or individual conferences. For example, before sending students to work at stations, ask them to look over their learning profiles and talk to a partner about the choices they plan to make that day. Have one-on-one conversations with students to address specific content needs and to revisit their profiles, reminding students of the importance of making appropriate choices as learners.

As the teacher, you also reserve the right to limit choices for a particular student at certain times during the school year as needed. If a student struggles with pacing or regularly chooses places to work that make it difficult for her to concentrate, don't leave the student to flounder on her own. Intervene and provide more guidance or fewer choices if needed. Ultimately, rather than limiting student control, our goal is to empower students to own their learning. However, to get to a place where students can successfully steer their own learning, we must first provide scaffolding, modeling, and choice within boundaries. One way to provide this much-needed support is through a weekly reflection, such as the one in Figure 4.5 (see page 56). In addition to providing time for students to reflect individually, give students time to talk with others about their goals and reflections. I assure you that this will be time well spent.

Designing Personalized Pathways

One structure that enables a flexible, personalized learning environment is the use of personalized pathways that enable students to choose how to interact with content and demonstrate mastery of learning outcomes. Pathways provide multiple opportunities for student self-assessment, empowering students to take ownership and control the pace of their learning. Essentially, a personalized pathway

- is aligned with learning outcomes,

- includes a variety of learning tasks based on interest, readiness, and learning profile,

- allows students to choose tasks and work at their own paces,

- includes a mixture of face-to-face and online tasks,

- includes embedded formative assessment opportunities,

- allows students to move on to the next pathway when they're ready, and

- allows the teacher to gather ongoing assessment data and track student progress.

Figure 4.4 Learner Profile

Learner Profile

What are your hobbies?

Your answer

Which of the following do you feel you are best at?

○ Solving problems

○ Reading

○ Writing

○ Conducting science experiments

Which of the following do you enjoy?

☐ Working with a partner

☐ Working with a group

☐ Working with technology

☐ Working outside

What type of learning environment works best for you?

○ Quiet

○ Noisy

Figure 4.5 Learner Profile Weekly Reflection

Weekly Reflection

Color in your self-assessment score during Math time for each PL Profile:

PL Profile	Monday	Tuesday	Wednesday	Thursday	Friday
Collaboration I worked well with others.	☺ ☺ ☺	☺ ☺ ☺	☺ ☺ ☺	☺ ☺ ☺	☺ ☺ ☺
Academic Risk Taker I used class resources. I tried new ways before asking the teacher. I tackled challenges.	☺ ☺ ☺	☺ ☺ ☺	☺ ☺ ☺	☺ ☺ ☺	☺ ☺ ☺
Leader I get materials quickly. I clean up materials. I transition quietly.	☺ ☺ ☺	☺ ☺ ☺	☺ ☺ ☺	☺ ☺ ☺	☺ ☺ ☺
Self-Directed Learner I complete all activities. I stay focused on my goals.	☺ ☺ ☺	☺ ☺ ☺	☺ ☺ ☺	☺ ☺ ☺	☺ ☺ ☺

☺ ☺ ☺ – Super job!

☺ ☺ – Good job!

☺ – I'm going to keep working on it!

Designing and implementing pathways takes time and planning, but you will find that the investment is worth it. Personalized pathways shift how the teacher and students use their time in addition to shifting ownership of the learning experience. However, the process for using personalized pathways does not have to be any more time-consuming or taxing than traditional lesson planning processes. Consider the following process for designing and implementing personalized pathways:

1. Select content standards, and rewrite them in student-friendly language.
2. Design one pathway for each standard or for a grouping of closely related standards.

3. Include a variety of types of content and tasks from which students will choose. Use consistent language, structure, or symbols to help students easily identify and self-select tasks from the pathway.

4. Use a pre-assessment to determine what students already know and can do and identify the instructional support students will need.

5. Identify the concepts, skills, and strategies students will need to be successful on the pathway tasks, and plan small-group lessons and whole-group mini-lessons to teach these.

6. Include formative assessment checkpoints to help you and students analyze student progress and determine when additional support is needed.

7. Make sure all materials students will need (print, physical, or digital) are easily accessible and organized.

8. Teach and practice the routines and procedures that will help students manage their pathway time. (More to come later in this chapter.)

9. Make sure to have a few pathways designed to allow students to move forward at their own paces.

Notice that the teacher tasks involved in designing and implementing pathways—planning small-group lessons, designing face-to-face and online learning experiences, teaching procedures, designing formative assessments, analyzing student data—are not new or unique to personalized learning. These are planning processes elementary teachers already use on a regular basis. The key here is to shift how we think about using these experiences to give students more control over their learning and increase equity in learning outcomes. Rather than planning a whole-group lesson to teach a concept, the blended teacher uses a small-group lesson to target the specific students who need that support. Instead of giving a summative assessment to determine what students learned, the blended teacher gives a pre-assessment to design the most effective instruction and learning tasks. In the place of whole-class guided practice, the blended teacher allows students to select ways to engage with content and control the pace of their learning.

Teams of teachers—organized by grade level, subject area, or department—can collaborate to share the work of designing personalized pathways. Once the team agrees on a structure and common processes and procedures for implementing personalized pathways, the team can share the work and lighten the load for everyone. Over time, the team can build a database of pathways and tasks that can be used again and again.

Figure 4.6 Personalized Pathway for Second-Grade Math

2. NBT.8 PATHWAY		I can mentally add or subtract 10 or 100 to any given number.	

Name: _____

Select 2 choices in each row and have your teacher sign off before moving to the next step!

Teacher Checkpoint	*I learn better by listening.*	*I learn better by seeing.*	*I learn better by writing/creating.*
_____ Small Group _____ Conference _____ Checkpoint Score	Watch at least one of the videos in the top row. [QR code] Write down 3 things you learned and explain them to a partner. Partner I worked with: _____	Look at a 200's chart. How does this chart help you forward or backward by 10? What patterns do you notice when counting by 10's? Create a picture that shows your thinking!	Caroline is solving 72 + 10. She is using a hundred chart. She starts on 72 and counts 73, 74, 75, etc., until she gets to 82. Paul says there is an easier way to find the answer using the hundred chart. What do you think Paul will tell Caroline? Write a note explaining what you think Paul said!
_____ Small Group _____ Conference _____ Checkpoint Score	Watch at least one of the videos in the bottom row. [QR code] Create your own video to teach a partner using examples! Partner I worked with: _____	Use a hundreds chart to prove your work and play Race +10 game with a partner. [QR code] Write 2 things you notice when you add 10 to any number!	Starting at 765, how many groups of ten will you need to add to get to 805? Starting at 329, how many groups of hundred will you need to add to get to 929? Create your own set of 5 cards (index cards) with your own questions similar to the one given! Use any tools needed to solve your questions!

Note: QR codes in this example are non-functional, and are included to show how QR codes might be integrated into a pathway.

Source: Charlotte-Mecklenburg Schools Personalized Learning Department.

To help you envision how pathways might work in your classroom, let's look at some pathway examples for the blended elementary classroom (Figures 4.6 and 4.7). The general structure for these pathways was adapted from a template created by the Personalized Learning Department in Charlotte-Mecklenburg Schools in Charlotte, North Carolina. In these examples, look for the following features of a personalized pathway, and consider highlighting or circling each of these components:

- Content standard written in student-friendly language
- Opportunities for student choice
- Formative assessment opportunities
- Consistent language, structure, or notation
- Blend of digital and face-to-face learning experiences

Figure 4.7 Personalized Pathway for First-Grade Math

1.MD.1 Order 3 objects by length, compare lengths of 2 objects by using a 3rd object
1.MD.2 Use copies of the same object to measure a larger object
1.MD.3 Tell time to the hour

Name: _____

Select 2 choices in each row and have your teacher sign off before moving to the next row! Be sure to color the boxes that you have completed.

Teacher Checkpoint	Standard	I learn better by using hands on.	I learn better by using technology.	I learn better by practicing the skill.
Conference	1.MD.1	Comparing objects		Splash Math
_____	I can order	Interactive Math		
Checkpoint Score	3 objects by	Notebook		
☐ Passed	their length.	**Go look at example.	Listen to the video!	Go to number 4.2
☐ Not passed – Go back to complete the 3rd activity.		COPY.**	Use the i-nigma app!	Measurements
_____		Put items in correct pockets.		Order Objects by Length
Reassess Checkpoint Score				
☐ Still need small group				

Note: The QR code in this example is included to show how a QR code might be integrated into a pathway; it is not intended to be functional.
Source: Charlotte-Mecklenburg Schools Personalized Learning Department.

As with all blended learning methods, personalized pathways can take multiple formats. Some pathways are printed on paper, with students using a notebook or folder to organize their pathway print resources. Other pathways are designed online, with students accessing resources via a learning management system (LMS), such as Canvas, Schoology, or Blackboard, or via a document management system, such as Google Drive or Google Classroom (see Figures 4.8, 4.9, and 4.10 on the next page).

Whether students access the pathway on paper or online, as the definition of blended learning implies, some pathway materials will be physical while others will be digital. A pathway might direct students to use physical math manipulatives for one learning task and a blogging platform for another task. See Figures 4.11 and 4.12 (on pages 62 and 63) for a personalized pathway for sixth-grade English Language Arts and a digital version of this same pathway created in the Canvas LMS. A pathway such as the one in Figures 4.11 and 4.12 might take students anywhere from five to ten class periods to complete. Keep in mind that in a truly personalized learning environment, with students controlling their own pace, some learners will complete pathways more quickly than others will. Once a student completes a pathway, he or she should be able to move on to the next pathway or to a different task that is appropriate with his or her learning needs and learner profile.

Figure 4.8 Pathway tasks include a mix of digital tasks and tasks that allow students to move around the room and work collaboratively with others

Figure 4.9 Pathway tasks can include games and other collaborative opportunities

Figure 4.10 Digital pathway tasks allow students to receive immediate feedback

In a blended classroom, students should not be held back by other learners. Pathways provide a structure that makes it easy for teachers to manage a learning environment where students are working on different content standards at different paces.

FOR THE LOW-TECH CLASSROOM

Personalized learning is possible without a device for every student. Although technology tools can allow students to work at their own paces and receive immediate feedback on their progress, there are ways to provide personalized tasks that do not require devices. When students self-select their texts for independent reading, self-select topics for writer's workshops, and choose manipulatives for problem solving, they are making choices about their own learning. These sorts of tasks can be included in students' personalized pathways, alongside digital tasks that can work in a shared-device classroom or a technology lab. Be sure to include enough nondigital tasks for students to work on while they wait for a device to become available.

Making Pathways Work

As you might imagine, successful implementation of personalized pathways requires careful planning and intentional classroom management. Based on my experience working with teachers in blended settings, classroom management can make or break personalized learning. Poor management

Figure 4.11 Personalized Pathway for Sixth-Grade English Language Arts

6.RI.1 — I can reference texts and events, providing explicit evidence to support my inferences.

6.RI.2 — I can determine a central idea and how it develops with specific details.

Goal	Task Choice	Task Choice	Task Choice	Checkpoint
I can reference texts and events, providing explicit evidence to support my inferences.	Read two different articles about the same event. Summarize the key similarities and differences between the two authors' points of view. First, create a T-chart to list similarities and differences. Then, write a summary of key similarities and differences including at least three paragraphs. Support your summary with details from both texts.	Use Piktochart to create an infographic including key information about a current event. Read a minimum of two texts about the event. Your infographic must include at least one section containing your personal inferences about the event. (*What do you think is the backstory for the event? What are/were the motivations of the people involved? What do you think might happen next?*)	Watch two of the inferencing commercials on Canvas. Work with a partner to write a script for a commercial that you could use to teach your classmates about making inferences. Remember that your script should leave out some key details so that the viewers must infer. Once your script is approved by Mr. Mureno, record your commercial.	_____ Conference _____ Exit Ticket
I can determine a central idea and how it develops with specific details.	Annotate a text you selected on Tween Tribune. Your annotations must identify the central ideas as they develop through the text. In color, highlight specific details that relate to the central idea. Next to each piece of highlighted text, add a sticky note to explain how the details support development of the central idea.	Read two texts about the same topic or event on Tween Tribune. Create a double bubble mind map to identify the central ideas and key details from the two texts. The central idea from both texts should be similar. However, some key details will be similar and some will be different. Place key details from each text in the correct places on the double bubble map to represent similarities and differences.	With a partner, watch a TED Talk that has been approved by Mr. Mureno and linked to our Canvas site. Identify the central idea of the TED Talk. Work with your partner to create a presentation in Google Slides. On slide 1, identify the central idea. Create three additional slides that list specific evidence from the TED Talk to support the central idea. On your fifth slide, summarize in one brief paragraph how the central idea developed from the beginning to the end of the TED Talk.	_____ Conference _____ Exit Ticket
I can apply my understanding of key ideas, details, and central ideas in my writing and presentation.	Work in teams of three students to complete this project. Research a historical event that is interesting to you. Review at least five online and/or print sources. Complete a graphic organizer to identify the central idea and key details related to the event. From the graphic organizer, write a script for an imaginary news reporter who is covering the event. Create a newscast using the Touchcast app. Group members' roles: Videographer, Reporter, and Eyewitness.			_____ Self-Assess _____ Peer-Assess _____ Reflection

Source: Personalized pathway designed by author and 6th grade teacher Diego Mureno.

can lead a teacher to think that blended learning can't work, at least not in his or her classroom. Often, trouble with classroom management is the main reason why teachers give up on personalized pathways. We have to understand that this way of thinking is new for many of us and that students

Figure 4.12 Digital Personalized Pathway for Sixth-Grade English Language Arts

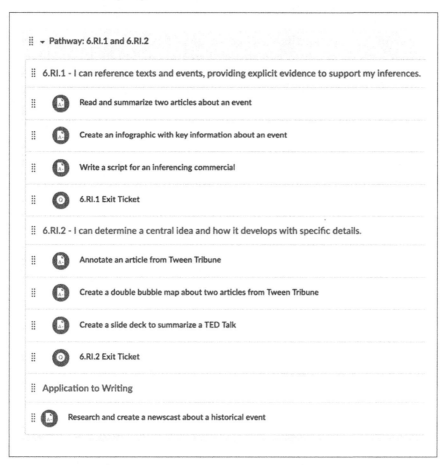

Source: Canvas, through Instructure.

are not used to having this much control of their learning. It takes time and intentional planning to make this shift work. Following are a few tips for making pathways work in your classroom:

- Use pre-assessments to allow students to self-assess and choose appropriate learning tasks

- Embed formative assessment opportunities for self-assessment and feedback for teacher and students

- Use symbols, icons, and consistent notation to help students navigate pathways

- Provide instructions and examples that students can access on their own

- Teach explicit mini-lessons about procedures for using pathways

I cannot stress enough that a personalized, flexible learning environment depends heavily on the establishment of routines and procedures. This may seem counterintuitive because the goal is flexible and personalized opportunities for students. However, to create an environment where students and teachers can manage and function effectively in a flexible environment, time must be devoted to the development of routines and procedures for governing personalized learning. Consider how the following procedures could be useful in designing and facilitating a personalized, flexible learning environment:

- Using data notebooks to select the most appropriate learning tasks

- Choosing where to work in the classroom

- Accessing and using digital and physical resources

- Getting help from the teacher or classmates when needed

- Managing time and tracking progress

- Choosing a partner for collaborative tasks

- Recording and tracking exit ticket data

- Providing meaningful peer feedback

Each of these procedures should be explicitly taught, modeled, and practiced using a gradual release model with the goal of student ownership over each routine and procedure. Time invested in teaching and practicing these procedures will be time well spent, enabling students to work efficiently as the year progresses. Without these procedures firmly in place, you will spend all of your time on managerial tasks. Transferring ownership of these procedures to students allows you to maximize students' time on task and frees time for you to provide targeted instruction and support. Once you and your students have these procedures firmly established, you will truly experience the power of implementing personalized pathways as students spend uninterrupted time on tasks that are just right for them and you spend time providing exactly what students need at the moment they need it. The following box includes a sample schedule of pathway time to demonstrate how the teacher and students might use time and resources as they work on pathways.

Scheduling Time for Pathways

- Project a list of which students are meeting with the teacher today for small groups and individual conferences.

- 5–7 minutes: Teacher teaches a short mini-lesson on a procedure or expectation related to pathways.

- 5 minutes: Teacher reminds students of where to locate resources for pathway and how to complete tasks. Reminds students of locations in the room for different types of tasks.

- Students pull up pathway on their devices or take out their pathway folders.

- 2 minutes: Students move to their work spot and begin work on pathways. Teacher plays a song or uses a timer.

- 7–10 minutes: Teacher pulls a small group for instruction related to the pathway standard.

- 5 minutes: Teacher holds conferences with students who have signed up.

- 7–10 minutes: Teacher pulls a small group for instruction related to the pathway standard.

- 5 minutes: Teacher holds conferences with students who have signed up or walks around the room to check in with students.

- Teacher continues to work with small groups or meet with individuals.

- 5 minutes: Wrap-up, reflect, goal-setting.

CLASSROOM MANAGEMENT IN THE BLENDED CLASSROOM

In addition to teaching, modeling, and practicing the procedures and routines listed in this chapter, consider leveraging another powerful strategy to help students take ownership of their learning: the classroom meeting. Classroom meetings are regularly scheduled whole-class conversations about issues related to the goings-on in the classroom. Typically, classroom meetings focus less on academics and more on procedures and *ways to be* in the classroom. Ideally, classroom meetings should be student-led, but early on in the school year, the teacher must begin by modeling how to facilitate a productive and kind conversation. My favorite resource for getting started with classroom meetings is *Ways We Want Our Class to Be* from the Child Development Project. A weekly classroom meeting can be a place where students tackle issues such as distractive behavior, inappropriate use of devices, respecting others online, and other issues that people encounter when they spend hours each day together.

Designing the Blueprint

Before moving on to Chapter 5, take some time to reflect on the personalized learning strategies and ideas described here. You may want to reflect about these ideas in a journal or blog. As you reflect, consider how you might shift toward a more personalized environment for students. Your shift to personalized learning might start with any of these tasks:

- Look for opportunities to use existing lessons, tasks, and assessments in a more personalized way.

- Create a plan for getting to know your students better.

- Talk with your colleagues about sharing the work in designing pathways.

- Identify procedures to establish, teach, and practice.

Complete the *Making It Personal* section of the blended learning blueprint to identify possibilities and starting points for personalized learning in your blended classroom.

3. Making It Personal

a. How can you move from differentiated instruction toward personalized learning?	b. How might you structure personalized pathways?
c. How can you give students control over time, place, path, and pace?	d. What routines and procedures do you need to establish, teach, and practice?
e. What will be the teacher's role as students work on pathway tasks?	f. What challenges do you anticipate? How might you solve them?

CHAPTER 5

Empowering Students

In this chapter, we will explore the following strategies for empowering students:

- Leveraging formative assessments

- Managing data and goal-setting

- Tapping into student passions

By the end of this chapter, you will be able to complete the *Empowering Students* section of your blended learning blueprint and answer the following questions:

- In what ways do students have agency over their learning?

- What are opportunities for increasing student agency and empowerment?

- How can you leverage assessments to help students make learning decisions?

- What structures and processes can help students manage data and set goals?

- How can you authentically model data tracking and goal-setting?

- How can you tap into students' interests and passions?

We've briefly discussed the importance of assessments at several points throughout the first few chapters, but it's time now to take a deep dive into the role assessments play in the blended elementary classroom. The key to using assessments in a blended classroom is to transfer ownership of assessment data to students. In most elementary classrooms, the teacher owns formative assessment data and uses those data to make instructional decisions. The next step for the blended elementary teacher is to work to help students track their own data and use them to make decisions about learning.

I previously stressed that one of the greatest benefits of blended learning is the teacher's ability to be more responsive to student needs. This is one of the most powerful ways technology can transform the learning experience for students. To be more responsive, in a systematic way, to student learning, we must begin by rethinking assumptions about how learning happens. The following assumptions about teaching and learning could provide a starting place for transformative conversations about teaching and learning. Blended learning can be the method whereby these assumptions are challenged and changed:

- Learning happens only in the classroom.

- The teacher is the sole source of content.

- All students should learn at the same pace.

- Students learn best when content is isolated into distinct subjects and class periods.

- Students should be able to demonstrate proficiency in the same way.

- Common pacing is the best way to ensure accountability.

- Student movement and noise are indicators of a lack of student learning.

- Students who are _____ [young, immature, disabled, language learners] cannot make decisions about their own learning pathways.

- A set of "best" teaching practices should work in all classrooms for all learners.

Rethinking these assumptions can help us approach assessment not as a "gotcha" or an afterthought but as a way to transfer ownership of the learning experience to students. In this chapter, we'll explore tools and processes for making this shift. Once students own their data and know how to use them, they are more empowered to control their learning and make choices in the classroom that are best for them.

Leveraging Formative Assessments

Formative assessments are ongoing, often informal opportunities to determine what students know and can do in relation to learning outcomes. Rather than waiting until the end of a chunk of instruction, formative assessments allow us to check on student progress along the way. So much of what we have explored so far in this book hinges on the frequent use of formative assessments. Without ongoing formative assessments, teachers will be unable to adapt instruction to meet student needs or plan small-group and individual supports. And without formative assessments, students will be unable to monitor their own progress, set goals, and make appropriate choices about learning tasks.

Countless tools are available to enable blended teachers to initiate change in response to student needs and progress. These tools make it easy to collect and analyze data about student learning and make immediate adjustments to instruction and learning pathways. In Table 5.1, I have listed several user-friendly and functional tools that can be an integral part of a blended elementary classroom, helping teachers leverage technology to be more responsive to student needs.

Table 5.1 Tools for Analyzing Student Progress and Responding to Student Needs

Tool	Using the Tool to Respond to Student Needs
Formative goformative.com	Formative is an assessment tool that allows teachers to design and deliver digital assessments and give real-time feedback as students progress through an assessment. One thing that sets Formative apart from other tools is the teacher's ability to turn a formative assessment into a two-way conversation by providing real-time feedback and replies between teacher and student. Another useful feature allows teachers to upload an existing document and quickly convert it to a digital assessment by overlaying assessment items onto the document.
Front Row Education frontrowed.com	Front Row is a digital assessment tool for language arts and math, designed for use in a whole-group, small-group, or individual setting. One helpful feature assists teachers with forming flexible groups based on assessment data. Front Row makes it easy for teachers to plan targeted small-group instruction, which is a powerful component of a blended classroom. The flexibility in delivery accommodates any blended learning model.
Khan Academy khanacademy.org	Khan Academy provides self-paced learning resources on a variety of topics encompassing math, science, history, economics, and computer science. Students in blended classrooms can work at their own paces with Khan Academy as one element of their personalized pathways. The teacher dashboard allows the teacher to easily analyze student needs by skill and intervene when needed. Students also can access their own learning histories and make choices about when and how to engage with content.

(Continued)

Table 5.1 (Continued)

Tool	Using the Tool to Respond to Student Needs
Plickers plickers.com	Plickers is a low-tech digital assessment option for blended classrooms with limited access to devices. The teacher uses a mobile device to deliver an assessment and gather instant results. Students use cards (printed or purchased from plickers.com) to respond to multiple-choice items. Real-time results on the teacher's mobile device enable teachers to make immediate adjustments to instruction.
Nearpod nearpod.com	Nearpod seamlessly integrates instruction and assessment, allowing the teacher to design interactive multimedia learning experiences delivered in a teacher- or student-paced format. When the teacher controls the pace, adjustments can be made to instruction immediately based on student responses. When students control the pace, they are able to rewind and review content and spend more or less time on specific content as needed. Nearpod essentially enables a teacher to "clone" himself or herself, facilitating multiple targeted small-group lessons at once. For example, the teacher can provide face-to-face instruction to one small group while other small groups are each working through Nearpod lessons designed for their own unique learning needs.
Quizlet Live quizlet.com	Quizlet is a study and quizzing tool that allows teachers or students to create and practice question sets. The basic feature of Quizlet is essentially a digital flash card tool. However, a newer feature called Quizlet Live allows teachers to design a collaborative learning experience, with students forced to rely on their teammates to review key content. When students complete a Quizlet Live assignment, the teacher receives instant feedback about the overall strengths and needs of the class as well as specific information about skills where students may need additional instruction.
Seesaw web.seesaw.me	Seesaw is a digital portfolio tool that allows students to upload evidence of learning through a mobile app. Students can upload photos, videos, drawings, notes, and links and annotate their work to reflect on their progress. Teachers and students can quickly and easily view changes in learning over time, and peers, teachers, and families can leave feedback on student artifacts. Seesaw also includes a blogging platform that allows even the youngest elementary students to blog. As a parent of two elementary-age children, I love being able to access their work in the app and leave comments for them.

In addition to increasing responsiveness in the moment, these tools enable teachers to be more responsive over time, archiving student learning data over days, weeks, and months. All the tools listed in Table 5.1 work across multiple devices. You can see some of these tools in action in Figures 5.1, 5.2, and 5.3. New tools are available on a regular basis, and the tools currently available are updated and changed frequently. By the time you read this, some of the tools listed here may even be outdated or surpassed in functionality. However, blended teachers should be self-directed learners, which includes taking initiative to identify, evaluate, and apply emerging technologies.

Figure 5.1 Kindergarten teacher Jessica Fitzgerald assesses early literacy skills and helps students track their own data in data notebooks

Figure 5.2 Students in Melissa White's fourth-grade classroom play Kahoot to collaboratively review math content

Figure 5.3 Students can upload a variety of artifacts of learning, and teachers can easily provide feedback on student work in Seesaw

Source: Jessica Fitzgerald's classroom Seesaw content from web.seesaw.me. Deacon Linton's student work.

FOR THE LOW-TECH CLASSROOM

Plickers is a low-tech digital assessment option for blended classrooms with limited access to devices. The teacher uses a mobile device to deliver an assessment and gather instant results. Students use cards (printed or purchased from plickers.com) to respond to multiple-choice items. Real-time results on the teacher's mobile device enable teachers to make immediate adjustments to instruction.

Managing Data and Goal-Setting

To help students manage their own data and set goals, teachers can support students by modeling this process with their own goals. At South Newton Elementary in Newton, North Carolina, teachers post their own Wildly Important Goals (WIGs) on chart paper in the classroom and regularly share updates about the progress they're making toward those goals. This transparency helps students see what it looks like to set a goal, track progress, and reflect on action steps. Don't let this goal-setting be a one-time event. Model how to regularly update your progress and reflect on what's working and what isn't.

In addition to modeling with personal goals, teachers can model the goal-setting and data collection process by being transparent with whole-class data. Consider creating a classroom data wall where you post data from whole-class assessments in the form of charts, tables, and graphs. Work with students to set goals and track the progress of the whole class. Celebrate when the class meets its goals, and help students identify which strategies and action steps helped the class make progress toward those goals.

Another support to help students with data management is the use of accountability partners. An accountability partner is someone who helps us stay focused on our goals and provides ongoing feedback, support, and encouragement. If you're like me, you may have experienced the power of having an accountability partner as you work toward your own important goals. Students can also benefit from working with an accountability partner, a peer who can provide ongoing encouragement and feedback as students work toward important academic, personal, and social goals. Schedule regular time for accountability partners to update one another about their progress, reflect on their goals, and set new goals.

Again, it would be helpful for you to model what it looks and sounds like to meet with an accountability partner. Model the types of things an accountability partner would say, and model how to respond to feedback from someone else. This type of modeling would work well using the fishbowl strategy, where you and your accountability partner sit in the middle of the classroom surrounded by students who observe silently. Following the role play, guide the class through a discussion about what they observed. Use this as an opportunity to develop guidelines and suggest conversation starters for accountability partners.

Student data notebooks are a widely used tool in blended elementary classrooms. These notebooks can be print or digital, allowing students to track multiple types of data, reflect on their progress, and set goals. Students might use a three-ring binder or a Google Drive folder. Either way, the key is to help students use data about their learning to take ownership of the learning experience. The student data notebook should be dynamic, with students entering new data, revising their goals, and reflecting on their progress toward goals on a regular basis. If students only use data notebooks once a quarter when they have new summative assessment data, we fail to empower students and transfer ownership of the learning experience. In a blended classroom, students should know where they are in relation to outcomes at any point in time.

There are almost endless possibilities for students to track meaningful data in the blended elementary classroom. Several data tracking templates are shared in Figures 5.4, 5.5, 5.6, and 5.7. Students might reflect and track data in the following ways:

- Update the learning profile as preferences change

- Reflect on work habits and set goals for managing work time

- Track pathway completion time and set goals for using time well

- Collect formative assessment data aligned with learning outcomes

- Track pre- and post-assessment data to show progress over time

- Reflect on which types of learning tasks help students learn the most

- Track dates and notes from conferences with the teacher

With the kindergarten data notebooking template in Figure 5.8 (on page 81), even our youngest students are able to track their progress toward end-of-year goals by coloring in the levels they have mastered. Think board game or racetrack. For example, there are thirty leveled sight word lists. When a student masters a particular list, she colors in the corresponding box on her data notebooking template to track her own progress. The goal is for each student to master all thirty sight word lists by the end of kindergarten and color in the entire track around standard K.RF.3 [Kindergarten, Reading Foundational Skills, Standard 3]. Students use the same process to track their progress with sight word phrases and reading levels. See examples in Figures 5.8 and 5.9.

Tapping Into Student Passions

A blended classroom provides a place for students to explore their own interests and passions. As students learn more about themselves as learners, they can use that information to engage in projects that matter to them. Blended elementary teachers can connect students with topics, community resources, and public audiences for student-directed learning. These projects might be connected to content standards, but they don't have to be. The key is that students follow their own passions and use what they learn to address real-world issues.

There are many different terms for this type of self-directed, authentic learning. *Genius hour, passion projects*, and *20 percent time* are all commonly used terms that refer to student-driven projects. Schools that implement genius hour typically provide one hour during the school week for students to explore topics that matter to them. This time usually results in

Figure 5.4 First-Grade Math Data Tracker

Operations and Algebraic Thinking				
Standard	**I can**	**Goal**	**Goal**	**Goal**
1.0A.1	I can use different strategies for addition to solve word problems (within 20).	☺	☺	☺
1.0A.1	I can use different strategies for subtraction to solve word problems (within 20).	☺	☺	☺
1.0A.2	I can solve word problems where I have to add three whole numbers.	☺	☺	☺
1.0A.3	I can use fact families to help me solve addition problems.	☺	☺	☺
1.0A.3	I can use addition facts I know well to help me solve problems where there are more than two numbers.	☺	☺	☺
1.0A.4	I can use what I know about addition facts to help me answer subtraction fact problems.	☺	☺	☺
1.0A.5	I can understand how counting up is like adding and counting down is like subtracting.	☺	☺	☺
1.0A.6	I can add facts within 20.	☺	☺	☺
1.0A.6	I can subtract facts within 20.	☺	☺	☺

Source: Created by Montclaire. This work by Charlotte-Mecklenburg Schools is licensed under a Creative Commons Attribution 4.0 International License. https://creativecommons.org/licenses/by/4.0. Based on a work at pl.cmslearns.org

Figure 5.5 Daily and Weekly Work Reflection Log

WORK REFLECTION LOG	Dates _____

Today I will accomplish
 	
_____
 	
Daily Reflection:
 	
   ❑ I accomplished my goal
   ❑ I conferenced with the teacher
   ❑ I learned in a small group today
 	
On a scale of 1–4, how would I rate today?
④   ③   ②   ①
	Today I will accomplish
	
	_____
	
	Daily Reflection:
	
	   ❑ I accomplished my goal
	   ❑ I conferenced with the teacher
	   ❑ I learned in a small group today
	
	On a scale of 1–4, how would I rate today?
	④ ③ ② ①

Today I will accomplish
 	
_____
 	
Daily Reflection:
 	
   ❑ I accomplished my goal
   ❑ I conferenced with the teacher
   ❑ I learned in a small group today
 	
On a scale of 1–4, how would I rate today?
④   ③   ②   ①
	Today I will accomplish
	
	_____
	
	Daily Reflection:
	
	   ❑ I accomplished my goal
	   ❑ I conferenced with the teacher
	   ❑ I learned in a small group today
	
	On a scale of 1–4, how would I rate today?
	④ ③ ② ①

Today I will accomplish
 	
_____
 	
Daily Reflection:
 	
   ❑ I accomplished my goal
   ❑ I conferenced with the teacher
   ❑ I learned in a small group today
 	
On a scale of 1–4, how would I rate today?
④   ③   ②   ①
	WEEKLY REFLECTION:

Figure 5.6 Fifth-Grade Data Tracker for Entrance and Exit Tickets

Fifth-Grade Entrance and Exit Tickets for Math												
Blue = 70% or Lower		Green = Between 71%-89%				Orange = 90% or Higher						
Standard		Date of Assessment										
S.NBT.1: Digit in 1 place is 10 times and 1/10 the value of surrounding places	Entrance											
	Exit											
S.NBT.2: Explain patterns in numbers of zeros by patterns of 10 (exponents and decimals)	Entrance											
	Exit											
S.NBT.5: Fluently multiply multi-digit whole numbers using standard algorithm	Entrance											
	Exit											
S.NBT.6: Find whole-number quotients up to 4-digit dividends and 2-digit divisors using strategies based on place value	Entrance											
	Exit											
S.MD.3: Recognize volume as an attribute of solid figures and understand concepts of volume measurement	Entrance											
	Exit											
S.MD.4: Measure volumes by counting unit cubes, cubic cm, ft, in, and improvised units	Entrance											
	Exit											
S.MD.5: Relate volume to the operations of multiplication and addition to solve real-world and mathematical problems involving volume	Entrance											
	Exit											

Source: Created by Smithfield Elementary School. This work by Charlotte-Mecklenburg Schools is licensed under a Creative Commons Attribution 4.0 International License. https://creativecommons.org/licenses/by/4.0/. Based on a work at pl.cmslearns.org

Figure 5.7 Fourth-Grade Student Data Tracker for Math

Name:	Student Data Tracker for Our Fraction Unit				
	"I can order fractions and explain when and how they are equivalent or their relationship."				
Standard	Pre-Test Score	Checkpoint Score	Checkpoint Score	Post-Test Score	Reflect on your progress with this standard. How do you feel/what do you think about your growth?
4.NF.1 I can create and explain equivalent fractions using visual models. I can create and explain equivalent fractions even though the number and size of the parts of the fraction may change.	4/5				
4.NF.2 I can compare two fractions by creating common numerators or common denominators, and using a benchmark fraction. I can explain why fraction comparisons are only valid when they refer to the same whole. I can correctly record the comparison of fractions using <, >, and =, and I can defend my answers.	1/4				

Pre-Test Reflection:	
Which standard/skill do you feel is your strongest based on your data?	
Which standard/skill do you need more practice with based on your data?	
Based on your data, what are your goals for this unit?	
How will you reach these goals?	
How will you know when you have achieved your goals?	

Source: Adapted from 4th grade at Oakhurst Elementary. This work by Charlotte-Mecklenburg Schools is licensed under a Creative Commons Attribution 4.0 International License. https://creativecommons.org/licenses/by/4.0/. Based on a work at pl.cmslearns.org

Figure 5.8 Shuford Elementary Kindergarten Student Data Notebooking Template

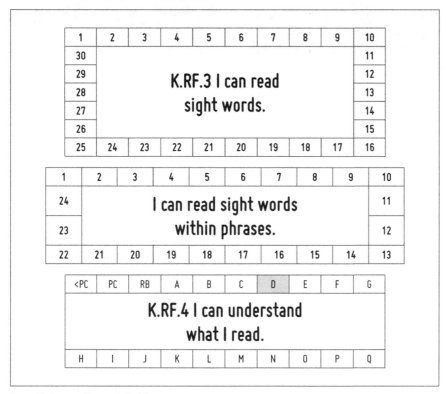

Source: Kindergarten Team at Shuford Elementary.

some sort of finished product or presentation. Passion projects empower students to research topics that matter to them, solve real-world problems, and meet community needs. The 20 percent time model was adapted from Google's philosophy that encourages employees to spend 20 percent of their workweek engaging in projects that aren't part of their normal job responsibilities but could benefit the organization in some way. In blended classrooms, the 20 percent time approach allows students to spend 20 percent of their time on self-directed projects. Structures such as passion projects, genius hour, and 20 percent time honor what students bring to the classroom and connect students with real-life issues that matter to them.

The expedition planning guide in Figure 5.10 provides a place for students to map out their passion projects and hold themselves accountable for doing what they set out to do. Students identify the goals they hope to master, describe how they plan to meet those goals, and identify the most appropriate audience for their work. Perhaps most important, students develop a timeline (with teacher support) of the steps they will take and reflect on their progress throughout the project.

Figure 5.9 Data Tracker for Personalized Pathways

Learning Cycle 4						
Power Standard	Goal	PRE Assessment	Pathway Start Date	Pathway End Date	POST Assessment	Self-Reflection (1–4)
RL.4.3	I can describe a character, setting, or event in depth using specific details or evidence from the text.					
RL.4.4	I can determine the meaning of words and phrases that are used in a text, including those related to mythology characters.					
RL.4.6	I can compare and contrast the point of view of a story (first and third person).					
W.4.1 W.4.9	I can write an opinion piece on a topic or text and support with reasons and information. I can use information from text to support my reflection, analysis, and research.					

My Learning Cycle Goals and Reflection:	
Goals:	Evidence of Goals/Reflection:

Figure 5.10 Charlotte-Mecklenburg Schools Expedition Planning Guide for Students

Expedition Student Planning Guide		
Mastery Goals:		
Concept Connection:		
Product Proposal (What can I create for my audience to master my goals and connect to my concept?):		
My Questions (What information do I need? What question do I need to answer?):		
My Audience (Who will be the best audience for my work?):		
Action Plan:		
Action	Timeline	Reflection

Source: Charlotte-Mecklenburg Schools Personalized Learning Department. This work by Charlotte-Mecklenburg Schools is licensed under a Creative Commons Attribution 4.0 International License. https://creativecommons.org/licenses/by/4.0/. Based on a work at pl.cmslearns.org

I hope you can see why the blended elementary classroom is the perfect breeding ground for this sort of work. In these classrooms, students have learned to use time and resources flexibly and direct their own learning. Consider adding one of these approaches to your blended classroom model to help students develop agency, or the capacity to take purposeful initiative. After all, student agency is one of the driving goals of the blended classroom.

Designing the Blueprint

If we're honest, I think we would all admit that there is more we can do to empower students and help them develop a sense of agency as learners. The strategies presented in this chapter can help you transfer ownership of the learning experience to students. Reflect on what you're already doing to empower students, and identify changes you could make to help students direct their own learning. Complete the *Empowering Students* section of the blended learning blueprint to develop a plan for empowering students in your blended classroom.

4. Empowering Students

a. In what ways do students have agency over their learning?	b. What are opportunities for increasing student agency and empowerment?
c. How can you leverage assessments to help students make learning decisions?	d. What structures and processes can help students manage data and set goals?
e. How can you authentically model data tracking and goal-setting?	f. How can you tap into students' interests and passions?

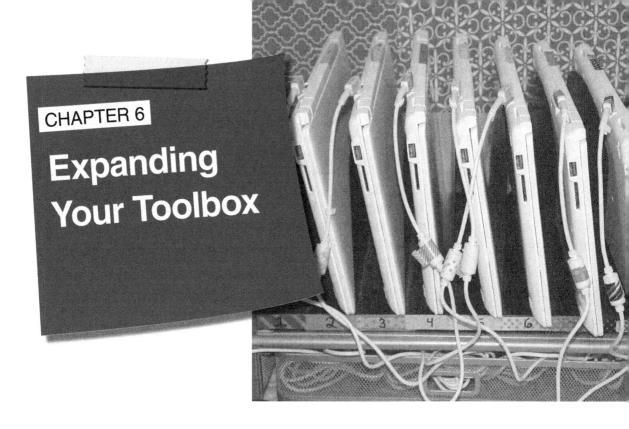

CHAPTER 6

Expanding Your Toolbox

In this chapter, we will explore the following ways to expand your toolbox:

- Designing collaborative learning experiences
- Leveraging adaptive tools for self-paced learning
- Amplifying student voice

By the end of this chapter, you will be able to complete the *Expanding Your Toolbox* section of your blended learning blueprint and answer the following questions:

- How can you leverage technology to create collaborative learning opportunities?
- How can you leverage technology to amplify student voice?
- How can students use technology to connect with an authentic audience?
- How can you leverage adaptive tools for self-paced learning?
- Which technologies best support your vision for blended learning?
- What criteria can help you evaluate new technologies?

One thing I love about the transition toward blended learning is that it forces us to think critically about the best use of face-to-face instruction and the best use of online instruction. As we have already seen, designing a blended learning experience involves maximizing the affordances of both face-to-face and online learning. Carelessly or randomly selecting face-to-face and online learning experiences does not exemplify the definition of blended learning cited in the Introduction. As a reminder, the Christensen Institute's definition of blended learning states, "The modalities along each student's learning path within a course or subject are connected to provide an integrated learning experience" (http://www.christenseninstitute.org/blended-learning-definitions-and-models).

This integrated learning experience depends on careful and intentional design and selection of the learning experiences that will take place online and off-line. This is central to the success of the blended learning experience. Teachers, schools, and districts must be willing to rethink how they use instructional time to strike the best balance between face-to-face and online learning. We must consider where we, as teachers, can have the greatest impact and where technology can have the greatest impact.

Just as we must be intentional about our selection and facilitation of teaching practices, we must also be intentional about evaluating and using technologies to help us carry out our vision for blended learning. I have said this before, but I'll say it again because it's worth repeating: blended learning is a means to an end. It's a method to help us and our students reach important outcomes. In the same way, technology is a means to an end. In a blended classroom, technology is a tool that makes new things possible for us as teachers and for our students as learners. In this chapter, you will explore technologies for teaching and learning that can be leveraged as powerful tools in the blended elementary classroom. You will also develop your own framework for evaluating the usefulness of new tools you will surely encounter.

Designing Collaborative Learning Experiences

As students take more ownership of their learning in the blended elementary classroom, this ownership applies to both their individual work and their collaborative work. The blended classroom is a great context for students to develop skills for effective collaboration and communication. For the blended elementary teacher to devote extensive time to teaching through small-group lessons and individual conferences, students must be able to manage work time on their own. This includes collaborative learning experiences. Too often, teachers give up on collaborative learning when students make poor choices or struggle working as a group. We must keep in mind that collaborative skills need to be taught and practiced, just as we teach and practice academic skills. You can see examples of elementary students working collaboratively in a blended classroom in Figures 6.1 and 6.2 and a collaborative student work sample in Figure 6.3.

Figure 6.1 The Shuford Elementary School kindergarten team showcases ways students use various tools in their blended classrooms

Figure 6.2 Fifth-grade students in Caitlan Reese's classroom use Google Documents during station rotations to respond to texts

Figure 6.3 Fourth-grade students worked collaboratively to research metamorphic rocks and create this informative writing in Google Drive

Metamorphic Rocks

By: Aspen, Annie, Zack and Hayden

Metamorphic rocks are changed by heat and pressure. They used to be sedimentary or igneous rocks! You will learn about all the rocks that are classified as metamorphic.

 Types of Metamorphic Rocks

Types of rocks that are metamorphic are: gneiss, marble and slate. Heat and pressure make up metamorphic rocks. If metamorphic rocks are melted, it makes magma. When the magma cools quickly it creates igneous rocks. If it erodes, it turns to sediments. Then the sediments have to compact to make sedimentary rocks. Then the sedimentary rocks have to have heat and pressure to turn into metamorphic rocks.

These rocks are constantly changing. Heat, pressure, and chemical processes change different rocks. Weathering and erosion break down rocks and move them from one place to another. The natural forces that cause weathering and erosion are always changing the rocks. Wind and water are breaking rocks into small pieces and moving them away.

A whole-group project is a good place to begin developing collaborative skills. In a whole-group context, you can establish, teach, role-play, and practice skills for working together effectively in a safe environment. Begin by asking students to reflect on their past collaborative experiences and share what worked and what didn't. Even our youngest students have had experiences working with others in some capacity. Brainstorm a list of guidelines for collaborative learning, and give students multiple opportunities to practice these skills and receive feedback from you and their peers. Consider developing a simple student-friendly rubric or checklist they can use during collaborative learning for self-assessment and peer evaluation. It can be as simple as the checklist in Figure 6.4.

Many collaborative learning strategies work well in a blended elementary classroom. I have listed my favorite go-to strategies in Table 6.1, along with instructions for implementation and possible tools for facilitating the strategies in a blended classroom. These strategies can work with all grade levels in any content area. Each of the collaborative learning strategies listed in Table 6.1 could be used effectively as completely face-to-face, completely online, or blended activities. In a blended elementary classroom, however, much of the collaboration would likely occur face-to-face, with digital tools serving as a way for groups to document, archive, and share their work. You may want first to teach and practice these strategies using the fishbowl method. For the fishbowl, you and one group of students would model the strategy while the rest of the class quietly observes. Afterward, facilitate a whole-class discussion about what students observed.

Google Drive is one of the most functional tools available for collaborative learning in the blended elementary classroom, particularly in districts that use Google Suite for Education. Students can use Google Drive on any device, and the commenting feature makes it easy for peers to give feedback, ask questions, and share ideas. The revision history feature allows teachers and students to see how student work has changed over time and analyze individual student contributions to collaborative projects. Another benefit of Google Drive is that it enables students to collaborate synchronously (in real time) or asynchronously (on their own time), making Google Drive a good fit regardless of your blended learning model. See Table 6.2 for a description of some ways Google Drive can support collaborative learning in the blended classroom.

Leveraging Adaptive Tools for Self-Paced Learning

With these tools, students are able to work on tasks designed or selected specifically for them and move forward at their own paces, while the teacher monitors student progress and provides intervention and enrichment as needed. This is the epitome of the power of the blended learning classroom: teachers let technology do what it does well so teachers can do what they do

Figure 6.4 Collaborative Learning Self-Assessment

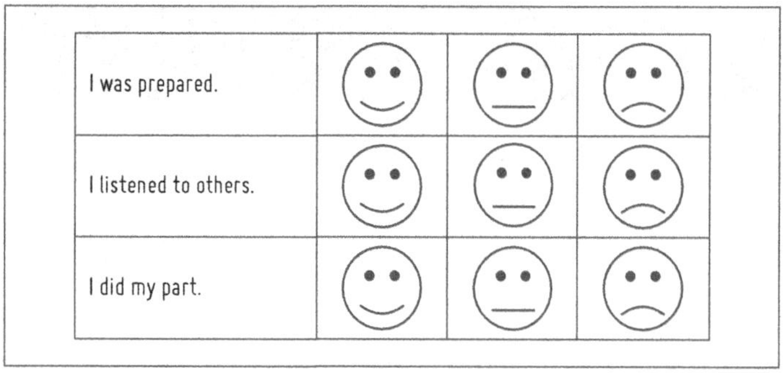

Source: Charlotte-Mecklenburg Schools Personalized Learning Department.

Table 6.1   Strategies for Collaborative Learning in the Blended Elementary Classroom

Collaborative Strategy	Instructions	Possible Tools
Jigsaw	1. Divide students into small groups. Each small group closely examines a text, concept, or skill so that all group members become an "expert." (Groups: AAA, BBB, CCC) 2. Mix groups for peer teaching. Make sure that each group includes at least one person from each of the previous groups. (Groups: ABC, ABC, ABC) 3. Each student must teach the other members of his or her new group about the text, concept, or skill from the original "expert" group. All students gain some exposure to every text, concept, or skill.	Google Slides, Google Document, Google Spreadsheet, Flipgrid, Padlet, discussion board
Think-Write-Pair-Share	1. Provide a prompt, topic, or question. Ask students to think quietly about the topic provided. 2. Students write (or type) their initial reactions and thoughts after approximately a minute of quiet processing time. 3. In pairs, students share what they wrote. Each partner has time to share and to comment on his or her peers' ideas. 4. Partner groups share what they discussed with the whole class or a larger group.	Google Document, blog
4-2-1-Freewrite	1. Each individual student brainstorms a list of the four most important things related to a concept (e.g., four most important themes of a novel). 2. Place students into pairs. Each partner shares his or her list of four, and the pair narrows those lists to two agreed-upon items. 3. Partner groups combine into groups of four. Each partner group shares his or her list of two items with the new group of four, and the group narrows these lists to the single most important item, as agreed upon by the group. 4. Each student freewrites about the one agreed-upon item for two or three minutes.	Google Document, Google Spreadsheet, Google Slides, Padlet, discussion board
Gallery Walk	1. Place students into small groups. Each group completes an assigned task and creates a visual to represent their learning (e.g., create a flowchart for the story's main events; draw a visual way to solve the problem). 2. Groups rotate to view the other groups' creations, and students leave peer feedback. You could ask all students to walk around and view the other groups' work, or you could ask one student to remain with his or her group's work to answer questions as students rotate.	Google Slides, Google Drawing, Piktochart, Padlet, Flipgrid (for sharing asynchronously)

well. Students benefit when teachers leverage the affordances of technology to maximize the instruction they are able to provide to students.

One of my favorite adaptive tools for the blended classroom is Khan Academy. Subjects available through Khan Academy include math, science, history, computer science, grammar, art history, and others.

Table 6.2 Google Drive for Collaborative Learning

	Ideas for the Blended Elementary Classroom	Teacher Tips for Using Google Drive
Google Document	<ul><li>Collaborative note-taking</li><li>Project planning and archiving</li><li>Coauthoring</li><li>Reflection and goal-setting with accountability partner</li><li>Readers' response entries</li><li>Peer feedback</li><li>Think-write-pair-share</li><li>Collaborative brainstorming</li></ul>	<ul><li>Share assignments with students so they always have access to the content and instructions they need</li><li>Have students create folders and share them with you for access to works-in-progress</li></ul>
Google Slides	<ul><li>Peer teaching</li><li>Presentations to peers or authentic audience</li><li>Vocabulary: one slide per term</li><li>Jigsaw: one slide per group</li><li>Two-column shared notes</li></ul>	<ul><li>Use Google Slides to serve as a guide for student-led conferences</li><li>Create a template first and then have students make a copy</li></ul>
Google Forms	<ul><li>Formative assessment</li><li>Interest survey</li><li>Learner profile</li><li>Data collection for student-led research</li><li>Peer feedback</li></ul>	<ul><li>Design personalized formative assessments that adapt based on students' responses</li><li>Gather feedback about student learning preferences and quality of instruction</li></ul>
Google Spreadsheet	<ul><li>Project management</li><li>Peer feedback</li><li>Collaborative note-taking</li><li>Data analysis for student-led research</li></ul>	<ul><li>Assign each student a row or column to avoid accidental deletion of content</li><li>Share data about progress toward whole-class learning goals</li></ul>

Through Khan Academy, the teacher creates a class, adds students, and assigns content. Students then work through the assigned curriculum independently, completing tasks and earning points, badges, and avatars. When a student struggles with a task, Khan Academy assigns a video to provide instruction with the target skill. Khan Academy can work well for fully online learners, but I believe it is most effective in the blended classroom. As students complete tasks at their own paces, the teacher has access to real-time analytics that allow the teacher to intervene immediately and provide support when needed. Whole-class data can help the teacher identify trends and whole-group strengths and needs, and individual student data can help the teacher pinpoint student needs and provide targeted intervention. See Figures 6.5, 6.6, and 6.7 for sample teacher data from Khan Academy.

Figure 6.5 Khan Academy allows you to quickly identify which skills students have mastered or practiced and areas where students are struggling

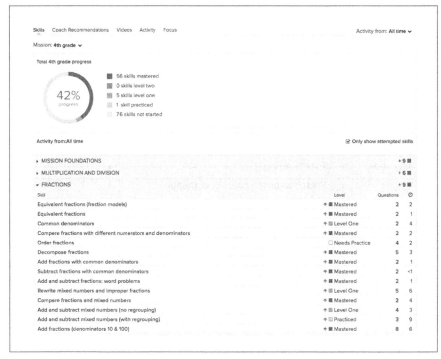

Source: KHAN ACADEMY® NOTE: All Khan Academy content is available for free at www.khanacademy.org

Figure 6.6 Khan Academy makes recommendations for each student based on individual data

Creating bar charts (+4 more)	Mastery Status	Questions	Goal
✓ Read bar graphs and solve 2 step problems	Mastered ▪	5	5 in a row ✕
✓ Create picture graphs (picture more than 1)	Mastered ▪	5	5 in a row ✕
✓ Solve problems with bar graphs 1	Practiced ▫	5	5 in a row ✕
✓ Solve problems with bar graphs 2	Practiced ▫	7	5 in a row ✕

Source: KHAN ACADEMY® NOTE: All Khan Academy content is available for free at www.khanacademy.org

A literacy tool for younger elementary students that works in a similar way is Teach Your Monster to Read, a free reading game from the Usborne Foundation. The game is designed for prekindergarten and kindergarten, helping students develop such skills as letter–sound correspondence, blending, and comprehension. Students work at their own paces and their own skill levels, and the game adjusts based on what students need. The teacher can track student progress and provide individual and small-group support

Figure 6.7 View a list of videos students have watched on Khan Academy to identify where students may be looking for support

Skills	Recommendations	**Videos**	Badges	Activity	Focus		
February 20, 2016		Reading bar charts: comparing two sets of data					1 minute
February 24, 2016		Rethinking three digit addition for mental calculation					3 minutes
May 17, 2016		Plotting basic fractions on the number line Recognizing fractions exercise Counting unit squares to find area formula					9 minutes
May 22, 2016		Mixed number or improper fraction on a number line Counting unit squares to find area formula					2 minutes
May 31, 2016		Area word problem: house size					3 minutes
Jul 29th		Time differences					4 minutes
May 30th		Naming angles Constructing angles Drawing parallel line segments					9 minutes

Source: KHAN ACADEMY® NOTE: All Khan Academy content is available for free at www.khanacademy.org

Figure 6.8 Kindergarteners in Jessica Fitzgerald's classroom play Teach Your Monster to Read during literacy stations

as needed. Teach Your Monster to Read provides supplemental resources for the blended elementary classroom, including songs, tabletop games, posters, playing cards, and more (see Figure 6.8).

Front Row Education is an adaptive tool that provides interactive math, English language arts, and social studies practice for students. Students begin by completing a diagnostic assessment, then Front Row Education provides practice opportunities at each student's level, allowing them to work on what they need to work on and do so at their own pace. As with other adaptive programs, the teacher can track which standards students have mastered and provide instruction and support as needed. These technologies equip the blended elementary teacher to align instruction with the definition of blended learning, which includes student control over time, place, path, or pace and an integrated face-to-face and online learning experience.

FOR THE LOW-TECH CLASSROOM

If you want to take advantage of tools such as Khan Academy and Front Row Education for adaptive learning but don't have a device for every student, you may need to think creatively about scheduling. One option to give all students time for these tools is to use your regularly scheduled technology lab time. Have all students work through their next Khan Academy practice set when you visit the lab. Also seek out opportunities to check out any devices that are available, such as a mobile lab. If you have a few devices in your classroom, consider creating a weekly rotating schedule that provides each student with time to work on his her or personalized tasks. Finally, you may want to consider partnering students who have similar strengths and learning needs. You may be able to get more bang for your buck with devices if students work as partners.

Amplifying Student Voice

Blogging is one of the technologies I talk about most often with teachers. When teachers ask me questions such as these: How can students create digital science notebooks? My answer is blogging. How can I connect students with real reasons to write? Blogging. Learn to use evidence to support their thinking? Blogging. Learn to be kind and interact appropriately online? Blogging. This is the only place in the book where I will devote an entire section to one type of technology. That should tell you something about how much value I place on blogging as a tool for teaching and learning. Blogging has tremendous benefits for students, including these:

- An authentic audience for student work
- Exposure to diverse ideas and ways of thinking
- Documentation of student learning over time

Table 6.3 Blogging Tools for the Blended Elementary Classroom

Blogging Platform	Features
Seesaw	In addition to hosting digital portfolios for students, Seesaw offers a free class blogging platform. Once you enable Seesaw blogs, students can select work from their Seesaw portfolios to share on the class blog. Teachers can control who has access to student work, customize commenting options to protect student privacy, and connect students with other class blogs in Seesaw, all within a safe environment (see Figure 6.9).
Kidblog	Kidblog offers more blogging functionality, with an individual blog available for each student. In addition to text, students can embed photos, audio, and videos from any device. Teachers have complete control over sharing and commenting, which means student work remains private unless the teacher shares it publicly. Connect with other classes through the Kidblog network. Kidblog is a paid subscription service.
Edublogs	Edublogs is powered by WordPress, which gives it more functionality and customizable options than other student-friendly blogging platforms. Teachers moderate posts and comments and maintain control of privacy settings. For teaching through feedback, teachers can leave private comments on student blogs that are visible only to the blog author. You can set up student blogs for free or pay for an account with more storage space and enhanced features.
Blogger	Blogger is Google's free blogging platform. If your district uses Google Suite for Education, your Google administrator must first enable Blogger access at the district level. For students who use Google's tools on a regular basis, Blogger can provide ease of access and use. Writing a blog post is as simple as using a word-processing tool. As with the other blogging platforms shared here, the teacher can control privacy of blogs and posts.

- Opportunity to justify and provide evidence to support student thinking
- Opportunity to critique others' reasoning

Blogging provides a public space for students to share their work. However, blogs are not only useful for publishing finished products. Blogging can actually serve as part of the learning process. Students often need to talk or write to reach their best ideas. The act of writing can help our students clearly articulate their ideas, choose how best to represent their thoughts, and change their thinking as they work. Many times when I write, I stumble across new ideas or new ways to represent what I'm thinking. Our students can benefit from blogging in the same way.

You may be wondering if blogging can actually work in an elementary classroom. Actually, several blogging platforms are available and appropriate for the elementary classroom. These platforms allow the teacher to moderate student posts and control privacy of student work. Table 6.3 describes a few that are easy to use for even our youngest students.

You may choose to use blogging as one station in your station rotation model, or you may decide to help students craft their blog posts in a whole-group, small-group, or one-on-one setting. Just as with any new form of writing, begin with

Figure 6.9 Melissa White's fourth-grade students use Seesaw to document their learning over time

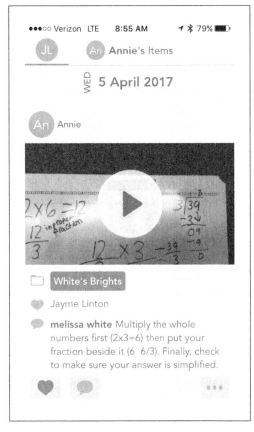

Source: Melissa White's classroom content on Seesaw, web.seesaw.me. Annie Linton's student work.

modeling and establishing expectations, then allow students to practice with guidance and feedback from you before moving toward independence. When you first introduce blogging to your class, create an anchor chart to demonstrate the various components of an exemplary blog post. Make time to revisit blogging expectations often, using student work to teach what to do and what not to do. Following are just a few ideas for blogging in the blended elementary classroom:

- *Use blogging for student math journals.* Have students solve problems, explain their reasoning, and demonstrate multiple strategies for thinking mathematically. Use peer commenting for students to critique the reasoning of others.

- *Use blogging for science notebooks.* Students can record their predictions, make observations, upload pictures and videos of their investigations, conduct research, and share findings. Use peer commenting for scientific inquiry and elaboration of findings.

- *Use blogging for the writing process.* A blog is a great place for publishing finished pieces of writing, and a blog can provide a space for students to document each step of the writing process: prewriting, drafting, revising, editing, and publishing. Use peer commenting for revision, editing, and public sharing.

- *Use blogging for reflection and goal-setting.* Students can use a blog as a digital portfolio, uploading multiple types of artifacts to represent their learning over time and justifying how each artifact connects with academic, social, or personal goals. Use peer commenting to provide feedback on student work.

As you can see, blogging can support many of your goals for student learning in the blended classroom. As with most of the other learning processes I have described in this book, it is important to begin by establishing and teaching specific procedures and expectations related to blogging.

Invest time in modeling and teaching how to use a blog, including how to leave meaningful and appropriate comments. You can expand the impact of blogging by connecting your students with other students who blog. Find other teachers who use blogging with students, and provide ongoing opportunities for students to read and comment on each other's blogs. This type of collaborative experience can help students develop academic skills and be better communicators and more culturally responsive citizens.

Designing the Blueprint

As a blended elementary teacher, you will no doubt encounter new tools on a weekly, sometimes daily basis. It can feel overwhelming to be faced with so many new tools. Keep in mind that the solution to issues we're facing in the classroom typically will not be found in technologies. If you and your students can accomplish what you need to accomplish with the tools you have, then there's no need to pressure yourself to master new tools on a regular basis. However, sometimes new technologies present new opportunities for the blended classroom that were not previously possible. It can be helpful to have a framework, or a way of thinking about new tools, to make it easy and efficient to evaluate new tools.

To develop such a framework, you will need to identify the most important criteria for new tools. These criteria will be different for each teacher and depend on your core values, your model of blended learning, and your priorities for teaching and learning. Consider the following criteria for evaluating the usefulness of new tools, and identify the ones that are most important for you and your students. Add criteria that may be missing. Narrow the list to a handful of criteria that can serve as lenses you use to evaluate the new tools you encounter. The tool:

- Is freely available

- Functions across multiple types of devices

- Is accessible for all learners

- Is easy to navigate

- Has no (or limited) advertisements

- Is equipped with a teacher dashboard or other process for teacher monitoring

- Has privacy settings that allow student and teacher to control sharing

- Does not require an email address

- Does not collect personal information from students

- Is on the district-approved list of websites for use in the classroom

5. Expanding Your Toolbox

a. How can you leverage technology to create collaborative learning opportunities?	b. How can you leverage technology to amplify student voice?

c. How can students use technology to connect with an authentic audience?	d. How can you leverage adaptive tools for self-paced learning?

e. Which technologies best support your vision for blended learning?	f. What criteria can help you evaluate new technologies?

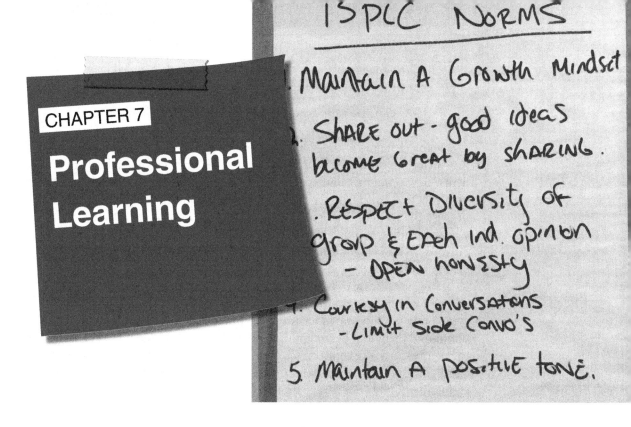

CHAPTER 7

Professional Learning

In this chapter, we will explore the following strategies for engaging in professional learning:

- Collaborating with colleagues

- Connecting with stakeholders

- Owning your professional learning

By the end of this chapter, you will be able to complete the *Professional Learning* section of your blended learning blueprint and answer the following questions:

- How can you leverage technology to connect with stakeholders?

- How can technology increase or improve your collaboration with colleagues?

- What technologies can you leverage for personalized professional learning?

- What are your professional learning needs related to blended and personalized learning?

- Who can support you with implementing your blended learning blueprint?

- How can you support other educators with blended learning?

Many elements of the blended learning transition can seem overwhelming, including the changing role of the teacher, the empowered role of students, new schedules and structures, new instructional strategies, revised data practices, and new technologies. Fear and uncertainty about any one of these changes could stop a blended learning transition in its tracks. Those who are leading blended learning in their classrooms, schools, and districts must expect a certain amount of ambiguity and be willing to implement change without knowing all the answers.

However, know that you do not have to do this work alone. An entire community of educators and other stakeholders wants to support you in carrying out your new vision for teaching and learning. You just have to reach out to find them and begin building relationships. This chapter is dedicated to helping you make connections with your local colleagues, with other educators beyond your local school or district, and with stakeholders in the community and beyond to support you and your students in this transition.

Collaborating With Colleagues

Your transition to blended learning can be supported by collaboration with other educators with a similar vision of teaching and learning. Working closely with a team of colleagues can save you time, provide you with feedback on your ideas, and benefit your students. The effectiveness of collaboration with your colleagues will depend on several factors: the relationship among members of your team, the culture of your school, the variance in instructional philosophies and practices among your team, and your own willingness and ability to lead. Consider your unique context. Rate your team (grade level, department, etc.) using the following continua. Consider how these various factors might influence collaboration among your team members and your own ability to take the initiative. In which of the following areas would you like to see change occur? What might be your role in that change?

Collaborative school culture	Competitive school culture
Transparency in teaching practice	Unwillingness to share teaching practice
Similar visions for teaching and learning	Opposing visions for teaching and learning

| Ample time and space for collaboration | | No time or space for collaboration |
| Focus on what's best for students | | Focus on what's best for teachers |

If you find that your context is not conducive to collaboration or your team is not accustomed to working together closely to improve learning for students, you may want to consider using protocols to provide opportunities for professional conversations. Protocols are structures that provide a safe environment for professional learning and critical conversations. In addition to providing a common language and way of thinking, protocols can provide structure for collaborative conversation and clarify the roles of everyone involved. The structure and common language provided by protocols can remove tension and help a team of teachers embrace and work through changes together. One of my favorite resources for protocols is *Protocols for Professional Learning,* by Lois Brown Easton (2009). The chapter on protocols for examining educator practice can be particularly helpful when transitioning to blended learning.

Protocols can provide a structure for honest, open dialogue about teaching practice. Consider using protocols to facilitate conversations about successes, failures, and challenges with your colleagues. Protocols support transparency by focusing the conversation on student work, removing some of the pressure and tension teachers feel when talking openly about their practice. As teams of teachers analyze student work with an eye toward how certain instructional moves influence student learning, the conversation shifts away from teachers toward students. This shift in professional dialogue among teachers can increase transparency and trust.

> Protocols can provide a structure for honest, open dialogue about teaching practice.

There is no shortage of digital tools available to facilitate collaboration among your team members and with educators beyond your school. New collaborative tools continue to become available, and existing tools are given regular updates and new features. The key to maximizing digital tools for collaboration lies not in becoming proficient with every new tool but in careful selection of tools that serve specific purposes. Identify your needs for collaboration among your local team members and with your online connections, and evaluate tools to determine which tools match those needs. Table 7.1 describes five popular collaborative tools, focusing specifically on how these tools can support collaboration among blended teachers.

Table 7.1 Tools for Blended Teacher Collaboration

Tool	Description	Blended Teacher Collaboration
Google Drive	Google Drive is a cloud-based, collaborative file storage system that allows users to create, access, edit, and share files from any Internet-enabled device.	Share the work of blended teaching by collaboratively developing personalized pathways and creating online content for blended learning. Use shared folders to organize content and share templates, tools, and resources with students.
Google Calendar	Google Calendar is a cloud-based, collaborative calendar tool that allows users to keep track of events from any Internet-enabled device.	Create a shared calendar for your team to schedule events such as common student assessments and team planning sessions. Add attachments and content to calendar invites to "flip" your team meetings, allowing members to preview content in advance.
Google Keep	Google Keep is a cloud-based, collaborative note-taking tool that allows users to create and share notes, lists, images, and audio from any Internet-enabled device.	Google Keep can help your team track to-do items, share photos from your classrooms, and communicate on the go with audio notes. Share successes and reach out for suggestions when things don't go well. Choose which notes to share with your team and which to keep private.
Diigo	Diigo is a cloud-based social bookmarking tool that enables users to share, annotate, and discuss web content from any Internet-enabled device (see Figure 7.1).	Create a Diigo Group for private sharing of web content among your blended team or a group of teachers you connect with globally. Members can annotate, tag, and discuss web resources that are useful in the blended classroom.
Slack	Slack is a cloud-based tool that facilitates communication among team members, providing space for whole-group communication and separate spaces for focused, small-group communication.	Use Slack to update your team members about the effectiveness of blended teaching strategies, share resources, and brainstorm ideas. For focused planning, sharing, and communication, create "teams" to divide your collaborative team into smaller groups by grade level, content area, blended model, etc.

Connecting With Stakeholders

I chose to include connecting with stakeholders in this chapter as a reminder that teachers can't do this work alone. Particularly in blended settings where technology is leveraged to meet student needs, collaboration with stakeholders can be a central facet of the learning experience. In addition to families, stakeholders include local businesses and nonprofits, colleges and universities, elected officials, and people who represent a variety of careers including scientists, librarians, museum curators, artisans, and others. You can create opportunities for students to connect, virtually and in person, with experts, community members, and other students. Multiple avenues exist for stakeholder collaboration and contribution in a blended elementary classroom, such as these:

- Ask stakeholders to record a short video on Flipgrid describing the role collaboration plays in their day-to-day work. Have students watch the videos, leave replies for the stakeholders, and write a

Figure 7.1 Members of a Diigo Group can share, discuss, and annotate websites

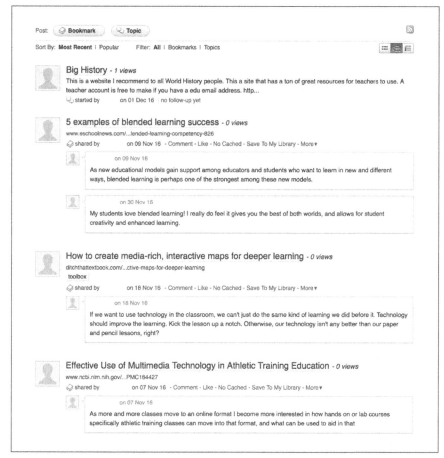

Source: Jayme Linton Diigo Group, created on Diigo.com

reflection about the importance of collaboration. You could repeat this same activity for a variety of topics, exploring the role of technology, math, or communication in various fields, for example.

- Invite stakeholders to serve as an authentic audience for student work. Local community members may be able to attend student presentations or meet with students in the classroom. Others can participate virtually by watching live presentations streamed online or leaving feedback on student work.

- Ask for help reading and commenting on student blogs. When students write for an audience other than the teacher and their peers, they tend to be more invested in the work and produce a higher quality of writing.

- Design a virtual student showcase, posting students' digital portfolios or artifacts of student work. Capture images and videos to bring the students' work to life. Or consider designing a reverse showcase, allowing stakeholders to share snippets (images, videos, products) from their careers or areas of study.

- Connect students with organizations in the community that are in need of volunteers. Schedule service opportunities and invite community members to work side-by-side with students, serving the community.

The iNACOL framework urges blended teachers to share their new visions of teaching and learning with their schools, communities, and the broader educational profession. As a teacher working to embrace and carry out a new vision with an orientation toward change and improvement, you have a tremendous opportunity to affect more than the students in your classroom. Here are a few ways you can contribute to the effectiveness and innovation of the profession, your school, and your community:

- Organize instructional rounds, or learning walks, in your school to provide an opportunity for teachers to learn from one another. Consider using one of the protocols for examining professional practice in Chapter 4 of Easton's *Protocols for Professional Learning* (2009).

- Facilitate a book study with other teachers in your school or district. Consider using this book or another resource mentioned in Appendix D: Recommended Reading.

- Connect your students with real needs in the community, allowing students to design solutions to actual problems faced by members of their community.

- Organize a parent night or a series of workshops to help parents understand the shifting role of the learner in a blended environment.

- Participate in a Twitter chat, an hour-long conversation focused on a specific educational topic. Visit www.cybraryman.com/chats .html for a schedule of educational Twitter chats.

- Sign up to attend an Edcamp, and take some colleagues with you.

- Organize an Edcamp for educators in your area. Visit www .edcamp.org/organize to learn more about becoming an organizer.

Owning Your Professional Learning

Just as technology affords new possibilities for student learning, new possibilities also exist for professional learning. No longer must teachers wait for a district-initiated workshop or a conference offered by a professional organization. Teachers can take control of their own professional learning, leveraging blended methods to design their own professional learning plans. Blended learning teachers have specific professional learning needs, represented by the iNACOL competency framework. Consider taking advantage of the opportunities presented in Table 7.2 for designing your own personalized professional learning experiences.

A network made up of educators from around the world can enable and empower blended teachers to connect with and learn from other blended teachers and educators with expertise in blended and personalized learning. In many cases, a blended teacher may be the only teacher in the school or even district using blended methods to personalize instruction for students. In these cases, blended teachers must actively seek out and develop connections with educators beyond the school and district to learn about strategies,

Table 7.2 Opportunities for Self-Directed Professional Learning

Professional Learning Opportunity	Description
Personal Learning Network	A personal learning network (PLN) is an informal, loose community of educators connected around similar interests and learning needs. Each educator can build and sustain his or her own PLN by connecting purposefully with other educators around common interests, instructional strategies, disciplines, etc. Members of a PLN are sometimes connected face-to-face but more often connected virtually via tools such as Twitter, Voxer, Google+, Facebook, and other social media platforms. A PLN allows educators to connect with others beyond the school or district to expand professional learning and collaborative opportunities.
Edcamp	Edcamps are free "unconferences," participant-driven professional learning events that typically occur on a Saturday. At an Edcamp, there is no predetermined schedule of session topics or presenters. Session topics and facilitators are determined at the start of the event, with participants voting to reach consensus on the most relevant professional learning needs. Blended learning is a common topic selected by Edcamp participants. Learning at Edcamp is active and happens through informal conversations and sharing among participants. Visit www.edcamp.org to learn more and find an Edcamp near you.
Action Research	Teachers transitioning to blended learning have a unique opportunity to analyze how changes in instructional practice affect student learning through action research. This method can provide a way for teachers to systematically gather and analyze data connecting student learning to teaching practice. This type of professional learning can focus on the specific learning needs of students in the blended classroom and enable teachers to demonstrate an orientation toward change and improvement.

models, routines, and resources that have led to successful implementation of blended learning.

Complex and meaningful collaboration can occur among educators who are at a distance from each other. If you have never experienced collaboration on a global scale, it may be difficult for you to imagine how this type of collaboration could be productive. However, I have experienced for myself the incredible power and impact of collaborating with educators with whom I originally connected online. Many of my colleagues and friends have also experienced the power in connecting and collaborating with other like-minded educators in diverse settings.

For me, collaboration with educators in my PLN is not something that exists outside of my work; it is an integral part of my work. I am a better educator because of my collaborative partnerships with members of my PLN. Following are a few of the ways collaboration with educators from my PLN has affected my practice. Each of these tasks was accomplished virtually, with educators I did not have access to locally:

- Collaboratively planned and facilitated professional learning opportunities for teachers

- Collaboratively developed syllabi for undergraduate and graduate courses

- Collaboratively conducted research and published articles

- Collaboratively developed content for teachers

- Collaboratively created curriculum alignment and pacing documents

- Collaboratively created personalized pathways for students

- Collaboratively developed student assessments

As you embark on this journey with blended learning in your classroom, invest time in establishing a network of educators willing to engage in shared practice together. This community can include mostly educators you connect with locally, mostly educators you've connected with globally, or a balance of them. Digital tools can facilitate transparency in practice, whether members of your community work across the hall or across the country from one another. In Table 7.3, I describe a few tools that can assist you in connecting with other educators for the purpose of providing and receiving support for blended learning.

Table 7.3 Tools for Building and Sustaining a Personal Learning Network

Tool	Building and Sustaining a Personal Learning Network
Twitter	Believe it or not, Twitter is being taken over by teachers. On any weeknight during the school year, you can find thousands of educators engaged in Twitter chats, one-hour discussions about topics of interest to them. Although many other tools are available for connecting with other educators and sustaining ongoing collaboration, Twitter often is the tool that facilitates initial connections among like-minded educators.
Voxer	Voxer is a free app and website that allows you to communicate asynchronously with others through text, voice, images, video, and attachments. One advantage to Voxer is its mobility. Members of a PLN can communicate whenever and wherever works best for them. Voxer allows teachers to easily share pictures of student work, short classroom videos, and text or audio reflections on their practice. The casual format of communication through Voxer can increase community among members. (See Figure 7.2.)
GroupMe	Another free app for communities is GroupMe, which can be particularly useful for organizing the work of a PLN. Members of a group in GroupMe can message the entire group or individual group members, using text messaging and attachments. GroupMe works very much like Voxer, without the voice-messaging feature.
Google Hangouts	For PLNs that are separated by distance, Google Hangouts provides a free space for synchronous communication with voice and video. Used through the website or app, Google Hangouts allows PLN members to connect in real time for open dialogue. Within a hangout, members can share documents or share their screens to increase transparency of teaching practice.
Google Drive	Google Drive is one of the most functional tools for shared practice within a PLN. Google Drive allows teachers to make their thinking visible, contributing to open dialogue about successes and failures. Teachers can edit shared documents in real time or asynchronously, with all members of the community having access to the most updated version of the document at any time.

Designing the Blueprint

I sometimes hear teachers complain that they don't know how to use a certain tool or strategy because they haven't been trained on it yet. Some elementary teachers may be thinking that they'll implement blended learning once their district provides some workshops. This passive mindset doesn't work for today's teachers or students. You can find an abundance of opportunities and resources available if you're just willing to look. Don't wait for professional development to come to you. Make your own professional learning opportunities, and make them be about what matters to you. Also, be on the lookout for opportunities to share your own knowledge and expertise with others. The fact that you're reading this book tells me that you already have a lot to offer other educators. Get connected and start sharing.

Figure 7.2 A Voxer group can serve as a space for you and your PLN to share strategies and resources, brainstorm solutions to challenges you face in the classroom, and reflect on your successes and failures

Source: Blended Practice using Voxer, voxer.com

6. Professional Learning

a. How can you leverage technology to connect with stakeholders?	b. How can technology increase or improve your collaboration with colleagues?
c. What technologies can you leverage for personalized professional learning?	d. What are your professional learning needs related to blended and personalized learning?
e. Who can support you with implementing your blended learning blueprint?	f. How can you support other educators with blended learning?

CHAPTER 8

Getting Started

In this chapter, we will explore the following strategies for getting started with blended learning:

- Starting small

- Planning for sustainability

By the end of this chapter, you will be able to complete the *Getting Started* section of your blended learning blueprint and answer the following questions:

- Based on your reflections and blueprint in Chapters 1 through 7, what are your next steps?

- What is a realistic timeline for implementing each section of your blueprint?

- What is your vision for blended learning in three months? Six months? One year? Two years?

- What challenges do you anticipate as you carry out your vision? Brainstorm solutions.

- What are possible indicators of success with blended learning implementation?

- How can you work to integrate students' face-to-face and digital learning?

By now, you have a blueprint that is nearly complete and full of ideas for moving forward with blended learning in your elementary classroom. You may be rethinking how you use formative assessment data, how you organize your classroom, and how you schedule the school day. Shifting toward student ownership and control of the learning experience requires us to make big and small changes and sustain those over time. I hope this book has given you more than just a collection of ideas for transitioning to blended learning—that it has given you energy to initiate and sustain change. As you have likely experienced in your professional and personal lives, change is hard. This chapter is dedicated to helping you identify what's next and begin implementing your new vision for teaching and learning.

Starting Small

Possibly the best advice I can give as you head out on this journey is to start small. Throughout this book, you have brainstormed action steps for moving forward with blended learning and designed a personalized blueprint for your own classroom. Know that it is entirely impossible and ineffective to make all of those changes at once. A successful transition toward a classroom culture that empowers students and provides equitable learning for all happens one small change at a time.

> Start small.

I encourage you to revisit the first six sections of your blended learning blueprint and rate each action step you've identified as a priority for you and your students. Rating your action steps can help you identify the greatest areas of need and the most important shifts that need to occur. Your ratings might look something like this:

1. Change daily schedule to make more time for individual and small-group instruction

2. Redesign the learning space to provide zones for different types of work

3. Establish procedures for managing independent work time

4. Talk with grade-level team about using personalized pathways for math

5. Set up student data notebooks/digital portfolios

Figure 8.1 Take advantage of a variety of spaces in the classroom to help you and your students organize and manage blended learning

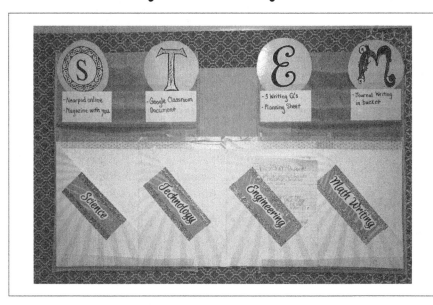

Starting small might mean focusing on the most important or the most reasonable change at the beginning of your transition. Starting small might mean focusing on blended learning in just one content area or one part of your school day. Whatever you choose, trust that small, incremental shifts will get you to your goal. Remember those core values from Chapter 2? Keep those front and center so that you don't lose sight of why you're making this shift. The pictures in Figures 8.1, 8.2, and 8.3 of blended elementary classrooms might represent appropriate first steps for you.

As you set goals and determine next steps for blended learning in your classroom, consider using a reflective protocol to identify opportunities for growth and action steps for change and improvement. One example is the coaching cycle, which is a process whereby a teacher identifies areas of strength and opportunities for growth, implementing action steps and gathering data to measure the change. Each cycle should aim for incremental change and last for approximately two to four weeks. This process should be teacher-initiated but can include others, such as peers, administrators, mentors, and instructional coaches. Collaborators can be particularly helpful in brainstorming strategies and assisting with data collection. Each coaching cycle should focus on a specific, actionable, measurable goal. Using the coaching cycle process for short-cycle growth and improvement can help you sustain your efforts by celebrating small wins along the way.

Figure 8.2 Organize materials for blended learning and teach students how to manage them

We use a similar coaching cycle process to support pre-service teachers at Lenoir-Rhyne University. See Figure 8.4 for a coaching cycle template you can use or adapt. A few possible focus areas for a blended learning coaching cycle include the following:

- Managing a blended learning environment

- Using data to personalize learning

- Providing timely, personalized feedback on student learning

- Using blended methods to provide immediate intervention

- Meeting diverse learning needs through personalized pathways

- Using blended methods to provide student choice

- Using blended methods to allow students to move at their own pace

- Using student data notebooking and goal-setting

Figure 8.3 Locate spaces in your classroom that can help you organize devices and other resources for blended learning

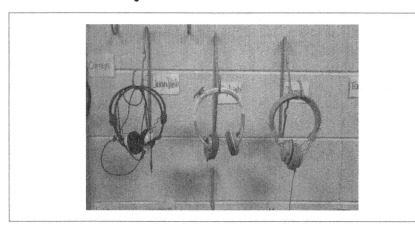

Figure 8.4 Coaching Cycle Template for Blended Teachers

Areas of Strength	
Mindsets • New vision for teaching and learning • Orientation toward change and improvement **Qualities** • Grit • Transparency • Collaboration	**Adaptive Skills** • Reflection • Continuous improvement and innovation • Communication **Technical Skills** • Data practices • Instructional strategies • Management of blended learning experience • Instructional tools
Focus Area for Growth and Development	**Action Steps for Change and Improvement**
Plan for Data Collection	**Results**
Future Goals / Next Steps	

Table 8.1 Sources of Data in a Blended Classroom

Data Source	What the Data Reveal	Possible Instructional Decision
Coaching cycle	Effectiveness of instructional strategies	Continue using an instructional strategy to maintain positive results
Formative assessments	Student progress toward learning outcomes	Plan small-group instruction to target a specific learning need
Informal observations	Student learning preferences Effectiveness of procedures Student ability to apply and transfer learning	Implement a new procedure to help students manage their time independently
Student portfolios	Student progress over time Student reflections on the learning experience	Help students with future goal-setting
Time for completion of personalized pathway	Student pacing Student time management	Hold an individual conference to provide a targeted intervention

The coaching cycle can facilitate short-term growth in blended teaching competencies, which over time can lead to long-term change. As you intentionally target your own professional learning needs and implement small changes in teaching and learning practices, you will continue to grow as a competent blended teacher. You may consider connecting the coaching cycle to your core beliefs, ensuring that your ongoing efforts to grow as a blended teacher are aligned with what you believe about teaching and learning. As you target specific components of blended learning in your classroom, you will need to gather data to determine which strategies are working and which aren't. Let's take a quick look at a few potential sources of data in the blended classroom that can help you continue to improve your blended approach (Table 8.1).

Data from these sources and others can be organized and displayed to facilitate analysis, reflection, and goal-setting. Many schools use data walls to visually display data. This transparent data sharing can help everyone stay focused on student results and provide an objective view of the learning experience. Each classroom can have its own data wall with class-specific data, whereas a school could have one or more data walls for school-level data. When implementing a new vision for teaching and learning, which involves changing practice and persevering through challenges, it is important to analyze results frequently to determine the impact of those changes. Blended teachers should take an objective view of data related to blended teaching so they can paint an accurate picture of the current reality of the learning environment in relation to desired results. An objective examination of results can help you persist toward your goals and make your vision a reality. Tracking progress (yours and your students') can make this change feel more manageable and help you sustain your efforts over the long haul.

Planning for Sustainability

Once you identify your priorities and determine which will be your first steps on this journey, it's time to think long term. Revisit your vision from Chapter 2, and consider breaking your vision into several measurable steps. What is your vision for blended learning in one month? What is your vision for three months down the road? Six months? One year? Two years? Be realistic about your goals. A realistic timeline for transitioning to a blended learning classroom is represented in Table 8.2.

One of the best ways to help you sustain your efforts along this journey is to celebrate small wins and successes. Take a moment to commend yourself and your students when you reach important milestones, of course, but also take time to recognize and reflect on the small changes that bring you closer to your goal. When you develop your first personalized pathway, that's a win. Celebrate! When your students independently manage stations for the first time while you work with small groups, track their first formative assessment data in their data notebooks, or meet with their accountability partners for the first time, recognize that those are important steps in the blended learning transition, and celebrate.

Regular written reflection about successes, failures, and challenges can be beneficial in sustaining you on this journey. For verbal processors, like myself, the act of putting your practice to words can lead you to better instructional decisions. Journaling or blogging can facilitate reflection on your practice, providing a space for you to evaluate your instruction and consider alternative strategies. Both journaling and blogging have their advantages by serving as spaces for private or public sharing, although the ability to connect with an audience of other educators makes blogging more conducive to transparent practice. Quite a few blogging platforms are available, each providing an

Table 8.2 Possible Timeline for a Blended Learning Transition

In One Month	In Three Months	In Six Months	In One Year	In Two Years
Identify blended learning model. Rework your schedule for the school day. Implement one new way students can make choices about their learning.	Begin teaching students how to manage data. Set up data notebooks for one subject area. Explore tools to help with blended transition.	Design personalized pathways for one subject area. Teach and practice procedures for student management. Implement adaptive tools for student pacing.	Redesign the learning space to reflect how you and your students use time and space in the classroom. Implement personalized pathways in a new subject area. Introduce students to blogging.	Tweak your blended learning model based on year one. Begin using digital portfolios. Implement personalized pathways in a new subject area. Design online content that allows you to clone yourself.

avenue for you to make your practice visible. Two commonly used blogging platforms are WordPress and Blogger.

Understandably, the changing mindsets of blended teachers described in Chapter 1 require persistence and sustained effort. As you change how you think about teaching and learning and work to redesign the learning experience for students, you will almost certainly face challenges. You must demonstrate—for yourself, your students, and your colleagues—that the vision is worth the struggle. Of course, there will be times you must react, in the moment, as you encounter new obstacles. However, rather than constantly reacting to challenges that arise, you can be proactive by anticipating potential obstacles, equipped with potential solutions. Table 8.3 includes a few of the barriers you may encounter as you implement a new vision for blended learning, along with possible solutions.

As a teacher educator, one of my favorite roles is supervising preservice teachers in their fieldwork, particularly supporting and coaching student teachers who are implementing blended learning in their placement classrooms. These teaching candidates are incredibly open to feedback and more than willing to make adjustments in response to their students' needs. I have seen them, time and again, demonstrate exceptional levels of grit in the midst of challenging situations. Following are two instances that exemplify how these incredible teachers developed solutions to complex obstacles:

- When students failed to show their work completely and accurately in their math pathway journals, one student teacher created a sample math journal and displayed it prominently in the classroom. She created a sample page for each pathway task to provide a model for the quality of work that was expected of students. (The student teacher and I first saw this strategy in action when visiting an art classroom at Grand Oak Elementary School in Charlotte-Mecklenburg Schools.)

- When students struggled to understand written instructions for pathway tasks, a student teacher recorded short screencast tutorials to model how to complete each task. The screencasts demonstrated for students how to navigate websites, interact with content, and submit their work. She then created a QR code linked to each screencast so that students could easily access the video tutorials using mobile devices.

In each of these situations, it would have been easy for the student teachers to become frustrated and give up on using personalized pathways in their classrooms. Grit and perseverance enabled them to see opportunities for improvement and implement change in response to student needs.

Table 8.3 Solutions to Common Obstacles in the Blended Classroom

Obstacle	Possible Solutions
Colleagues who are resistant to change	• Organize instructional rounds, or learning walks, to help teachers envision how blended learning could look in their classrooms • Collaboratively design personalized pathways to share the work of blended teaching • Use protocols to provide a safe structure for difficult conversations • Connect with other blended teachers beyond your school to build a network of support
School scheduling limitations that make it difficult to implement your desired blended learning model	• Share your concerns with your school's leadership team • Design interdisciplinary learning experiences to integrate multiple content areas in a single block of time • Think creatively about how you might adapt the blended model to fit within your scheduling constraints
Technical issues that limit your students' access to technology	• Empower your students to create a tech support team to provide tech help for their peers • Use a rotation model so some students need access to technology while others do not • Collaborate with your school's leadership team to promote a bring-your-own-device (BYOD) policy to increase access to devices
Classroom management issues that make flexible, personalized learning a challenge	• Explicitly teach, model, and practice procedures and routines needed to make blended learning more efficient • Create examples of student work, video tutorials, and other supports to provide scaffolding as students become more independent and empowered learners • Work with students to set goals and develop action plans related to work habits and time management

Designing the Blueprint

Keep in mind that change takes time. You may not see immediate, measurable results. (Remember that grit is a key quality of successful blended teachers.) Too often, teachers, schools, and districts abandon initiatives because they were believed to have little to no positive impact on student learning. Sometimes, abandoning ineffective practices is necessary. Many times, however, promising changes are abandoned before they're given ample time for success. We must remember that it takes time to carry out a new vision, to adjust to a new way of thinking. It takes time to change the culture of a classroom, a school, or a district. In blended learning environments, students need time to adjust to their new roles and take ownership of new procedures and processes.

As you set goals, collect data, and reflect on the impact of your instructional decisions, remember that this is an ongoing process of change and improvement. Your blueprint is not carved in stone. As culture or students or resources change, adapt right along with them. Also keep in mind that no two elementary teachers will implement blended learning in the same way. As you set out to use blended methods to help students take ownership of their learning, remember and trust that you know best how to take this blueprint off the page and build a culture for blended learning in your classroom. Own your journey, just as you aim to help students own theirs.

7. Getting Started

a. Based on your reflections in Chapters 1 through 7, what are your next steps?	b. What is a realistic timeline for implementing each section of your blueprint?
c. What is your vision for blended learning in three months? Six months? One year? Two years?	d. What challenges do you anticipate as you carry out your vision? Brainstorm solutions.
e. What are possible indicators of success with blended learning implementation?	f. How can you work to integrate students' face-to-face and digital learning?

Appendix A

Blueprint for Blended Learning

1. Crafting Your Vision	
a. What is your purpose? Why blended learning?	b. How can you adapt existing blended learning models for your own context?
c. What is the role of the teacher?	d. What is the role of the student?
e. What teaching practices are getting in the way of effective blended learning?	f. How can you redesign the learning space to support blended learning?

2. Maximizing Instructional Time	
a. What is the best way to use face-to-face instructional time?	b. What is the best way to use digital learning opportunities?
c. How can you rethink your daily/weekly schedule to leverage blended opportunities?	d. How can you think about content in a more interconnected way?
e. How can you "clone" yourself to provide multiple instances of targeted instruction?	f. What are some missed opportunities resulting from how you use instructional time?

3. Making It Personal	
a. How can you move from differentiated instruction toward personalized learning?	b. Sketch a design for personalized pathways.
c. How can you give students control over time, place, path, and pace?	d. What routines and procedures do you need to establish, teach, and practice?
e. What will be the teacher's role as students work on pathway tasks?	f. What challenges do you anticipate? How might you solve them?

4. Empowering Students	
a. In what ways do students have agency over their learning?	b. What are opportunities for increasing student agency and empowerment?
c. How can you leverage assessments to help students make learning decisions?	d. What structures and processes can help students manage data and set goals?
e. How can you authentically model data tracking and goal-setting?	f. How can you tap into students' interests and passions?

5. Expanding Your Toolbox	
a. How can you leverage technology to create collaborative learning opportunities?	b. How can you leverage technology to amplify student voice?
c. How can students use technology to connect with an authentic audience?	d. How can you leverage adaptive tools for self-paced learning?
e. Which technologies best support your vision for blended learning?	f. What criteria can help you evaluate new technologies?

6. Professional Learning	
a. How can you leverage technology to connect with stakeholders?	b. How can technology increase or improve your collaboration with colleagues?
c. What technologies can you leverage for personalized professional learning?	d. What are your professional learning needs related to blended and personalized learning?
e. Who can support you with implementing your blended learning blueprint?	f. How can you support other educators with blended learning?

7. Getting Started
a. Based on your reflections in Chapters 1 through 7, what are your next steps?	b. What is a realistic timeline for implementing each section of your blueprint?
c. What is your vision for blended learning in three months? Six months? One year? Two years?	d. What challenges do you anticipate as you carry out your vision? Brainstorm solutions.
e. What are possible indicators of success with blended learning implementation?	f. How can you work to integrate students' face-to-face and digital learning?

Appendix B

iNACOL Blended Learning Teacher Competency Framework

MINDSETS	What Core values or beliefs that guide thinking, behaviors, and actions that align with goals of educational change and mission How Understood, adopted, and committed to
QUALITIES	What Personal characteristics and patterns of behavior that help an educator make the transition to new ways of teaching and learning How Coached, encouraged, and reinforced
ADAPTIVE SKILLS	What Higher complexity that are generalized across domain/jobs. Help people tackle problems and tasks where the solution might be unknown or that require organizational learning and innovation How Developed through modeling, coaching, and reflective practice
TECHNICAL SKILLS	What Skills that are known and specific to task and domain. Observable "Know-how" and basic mechanics and expertise helpful for execution and implementation of day-to-day job (for teachers' instruction) How Acquired and mastered through instruction, training, and practice

Source: The International Association for K–12 Online Learning (iNACOL). 2014. iNACOL Blended Learning Teacher Competencies Framework. http://www.inacol.org/resource/inacol-blended-learning-teacher-competency-framework/

Appendix C

Reflecting on the iNACOL Blended Learning Teacher Competencies

As you work to develop the competencies needed for successful implementation of blended learning, where do your strengths lie? Which competencies are opportunities for growth? Which of these competencies can help you take blended learning to the next level in your classroom? Use the following tables to reflect on each competency and standard, identifying areas of strength and opportunities for growth. Along with each standard, you will find questions you can use to guide your own reflection and self-assessment. Consider using a digital journal or blog to make time and space for reflection as you design your blueprint.

Mindsets

Reflect on a New Vision for Teaching and Learning

Standard	Questions to Guide Reflection	Reflection
Standard A: **Shift from teacher-led instruction to student-centered learning** for the purposes of meeting individual needs and fostering engagement and motivation.	How can I include student choice and interests? How will students be active learners? How can I incorporate purposeful talk among learners? How will students use technology?	
Standard B: **Value collaboration** with various stakeholders to enhance student learning.	Who can support teaching and learning in my classroom? With whom could my students connect to extend their learning opportunities?	

(Continued)

Standard	Questions to Guide Reflection	Reflection
Standard C: **Create learning environments that are flexible and personalized**, dependent on real-time data, direct observation, and interaction with and feedback from students.	How might I reenvision this space? Where can I create flexible learning spaces? How can I involve students in redesigning the space?	
Standard D: **Model a growth orientation** toward learning for self and others.	What are my strengths? What can I improve? How can I foster a growth mindset in students? What language can I use to model a growth mindset?	
Standard E: Have an entrepreneurial spirit, and possess **creativity, imagination, and drive**.	What classroom procedure, concept, or idea can I approach in a different way?	

Reflect on an Orientation Toward Change and Improvement

Standard	Questions to Guide Reflection	Reflection
Standard A: **Embrace change** and model this for others.	What is not working well and how can I improve it? What new technique have I learned about but not tried?	
Standard B: Proactively **initiate change in response to students' needs** and progress.	According to data on student learning, what changes are needed? What practice do I need to add, change, or remove?	
Standard C: **Embrace uncertainty and ambiguity** as part of improving teacher and learning practices.	What am I wondering about my students? What is unclear? Who can help me see what I may be missing?	
Standard D: **Model** and encourage others to be **independent and self-directed learners**.	What are my personal and professional learning needs and interests? What resources and tools can I use to learn?	
Standard E: Demonstrate the professional responsibility to **contribute to the effectiveness, innovation, vitality, and self-renewal of the teaching profession**, as well as to their [teachers'] **school** and **community**.	How can I share what I am learning? How might my teaching practices affect the teaching of others? What do I need to share with my colleagues?	

Qualities

Reflecting on Grit

Standard	Questions to Guide Reflection	Reflection
Standard A: Engage in deliberate practice and **persevere toward ambitious, long-term educational and professional goals**.	What are my professional learning goals? What is my plan for accomplishing those goals? How can I share my goals with others? How might I overcome potential roadblocks and challenges?	
Standard B: Maintain and **model persistence, confidence, and optimism to resolve issues**.	What current challenge am I facing? What resources and strategies are available? How can I help others resolve issues?	

Reflecting on Transparency

Standard	Questions to Guide Reflection	Reflection
Standard A: Openly and frequently **share successes, failures, and challenges**.	What is working well and what isn't? How can I share my failures and successes with students and colleagues?	
Standard B: **Look objectively at all results** (both positive and negative), and help others to do the same.	What do the data reveal? What might I be missing in my data analysis? How can I help colleagues analyze results?	

Reflecting on Collaboration

Standard	Questions to Guide Reflection	Reflection
Standard A: **Balance individual initiative with teamwork** to accomplish organizational objectives.	What goals is my team working toward? What is my role in helping the team meet those goals? What can I contribute?	
Standard B: Proactively **seek to learn from and with other experts** in the field.	What face-to-face and online opportunities are available to learn from and alongside other educators?	

Adaptive Skills

Reflecting on Reflection

Standard	Questions to Guide Reflection	Reflection
Standard A: Continuously **take note of what is or is not working** (via student-level data, technology applications, pedagogical strategies, supervisor feedback, etc.) and **identify a plan of action**.	What do the data reveal about progress toward student learning goals? What data sources am I using? What additional data sources may be available? What should I celebrate? What are areas for improvement? What strategies can I implement to address those needs?	
Standard B: Collaboratively, transparently, and **proactively seek out feedback from students, parents, and colleagues** to continuously improve instruction and teaching practices.	How can I gather feedback on my teaching? Whose input do I currently have? What perspectives are missing?	
Standard C: **Apply lessons and takeaways about their** [teachers'] **own experiences as learners**, both online and offline, to their work with students.	How can my own learning experiences affect my instruction? What works for me as a learner? How might I use that in my teaching?	

Reflecting on Continuous Improvement and Innovation

Standard	Questions to Guide Reflection	Reflection
Standard A: Engage in **problem solving through continuous planning, designing, testing, evaluation, and recalibration** of teaching methods.	What new or revised teaching method have you used? What new or revised teaching method might you try? How have you/can you gather data to determine their effectiveness?	
Standard B: **Use technology creatively and purposefully** to work effectively and efficiently.	What technologies do you use to increase productivity, effectiveness, and efficiency? What process could you improve through technology?	

Reflecting on Communication

Standard	Questions to Guide Reflection	Reflection
Standard A: **Connect learners to sources of information** beyond the classroom teacher and textbook.	What sources of information do students have access to at school and outside school? How can I design learning opportunities to leverage those sources?	
Standard B: **Establish and maintain open communication channels**, online and in-person, with students, educators, and other stakeholders to support student learning.	What face-to-face and online communication channels do I and can I use with students, families, colleagues, and others? How can I leverage online communication for student learning?	

Technical Skills

Reflecting on Data Practices

Standard	Questions to Guide Reflection	Reflection
Standard A: **Use qualitative and quantitative data** to understand individual skills, gaps, strengths, weaknesses, interests, and aspirations of each student, and **use that information to personalize learning experiences**.	How do you gather ongoing data about student strengths, gaps, interests, and goals? How do you use that data to personalize learning experiences? What additional data sources might you use?	
Standard B: **Continually assess student progress against clearly defined standards, goals, and outcomes** to identify specific topics in which each student needs additional support to achieve mastery of a concept or skill.	How do you determine goals for student learning? How do you communicate those goals with students? What data do you use to assess progress toward those goals?	
Standard C: **Use data from multiple sources**, including data systems, in a complementary way to **inform and adjust individual student instruction and groupings**.	What do the data reveal about student learning? What are the learning needs of specific students and groups of students? How do I and can I use flexible grouping?	
Standard D: Create ways to **move ownership and analysis of data to students** to promote independent learning.	How are students involved in data collection and goal-setting? How do I share data about student learning with students? How can I move ownership of data to students?	
Standard E: **Continually evaluate technologies, tools, and instructional strategies** to ensure their effectiveness.	How do I determine the effectiveness of strategies and tools? Which strategies and tools are working and which are not?	

Reflecting on Instructional Strategies

Standard	Questions to Guide Reflection	Reflection
Standard A: Provide resources for students to learn content and **enable them to work independently and/or in cooperative groups**.	How do I use the learning management system to provide content? In what ways do students work independently and cooperatively? What new opportunities might I create for independent and collaborative learning?	
Standard B: Provide resources for students to **create evidence of their knowledge in a variety of formats** to demonstrate mastery.	How do students show what they know? How might I provide choice in how students show what they know?	
Standard C: **Create customized learning pathways with students**, where learning goals and objectives are linked to explicit and diverse learning experiences, matched to the individual student's learning performance level and preferences.	How is learning personalized for students? What is the role of students in developing individualized learning pathways? How can I create new, diverse pathways linked to individual students' learning needs and goals?	
Standard D: **Tailor content and instructional strategies to individual learning goals, needs, and interests**.	How are my instructional strategies matched to student learning needs, goals, and interests? How might I add more variety to my instructional strategies?	
Standard E: Create pedagogical approaches and learning experiences that **promote content-based problem solving and online collaboration**.	How often do my students engage in face-to-face and online collaborative problem solving? How might I use project-based learning to promote authentic problem solving and collaboration?	

Reflecting on Management of Blended Learning Experience

Standard	Questions to Guide Reflection	Reflection
Standard A: Understand and **manage the face-to-face and online components of lesson planning** and organization within a blended course.	What model of blended learning do I currently use? What management challenges do I face? How can I better manage face-to-face and online instruction?	
Standard B: Provide balanced opportunities for students to participate in **asynchronous and synchronous modalities**.	What synchronous and asynchronous tools would work well with my learners? How might I use them to provide opportunities for online discussions?	

Standard	Questions to Guide Reflection	Reflection
Standard C: **Develop, practice, model, and embody respectful behaviors** in both face-to-face and online learning environments.	How do you model and explicitly teach respectful behaviors face-to-face and online? What specific behaviors do your students need to learn?	
Standard D: **Demonstrate technical troubleshooting skills** during the online component of learning (e.g., change passwords, download plug-ins, etc.).	What potential technical difficulties may pose a challenge during online instruction? How can I proactively address those challenges?	

Reflecting on Instructional Tools

Standard	Questions to Guide Reflection	Reflection
Standard A: **Use learning management system and/or other online collaborative tools** to organize and manage the blended learning environment.	How am I currently using the learning management system and other online collaborative tools? How can these tools help me manage blended learning? What tools do I need to learn and implement?	
Standard B: Demonstrate skill in the **evaluation, selection, and use of effective instructional materials, tools, strategies, and resources for students**, and engage students in this process to help their achievement and development of academic skills.	How do I identify, evaluate, and use instructional strategies, materials, and tools? What should I consider when evaluating new strategies, materials, and tools? How can I involve students in this process?	
Standard C: **Provide assistive technologies** to facilitate learning.	What current learning needs should I address through assistive technologies? What assistive technologies are available to me? What assistive technologies do students need that are not currently available?	

Appendix D

Recommended Reading

Print Resources

- *Action Research: Improving Schools and Empowering Educators* (5th edition), by Craig A. Mertler

- *Blended: Using Disruptive Innovation to Improve Schools,* by Michael B. Horn and Heather Staker

- *Building Successful Communities of Practice,* by Emily Webber

- *Crucial Conversations,* by Kerry Patterson, Joseph Grenny, Ron McMillan, Al Switzler, and Laura Roppe

- *Grit: The Power of Passion and Perseverance,* by Angela Duckworth

- *How Children Succeed: Grit, Curiosity, and the Hidden Power of Character,* by Paul Tough

- *The Innovator's Mindset: Empower Learning, Unleash Talent, and Lead a Culture of Creativity,* by George Couros

- *Learning by Doing: A Handbook for Professional Learning Communities at Work,* by Richard DuFour, Rebecca DuFour, Robert Eaker, and Thomas W. Many

- *Mindset: The New Psychology of Success,* by Carol Dweck

- *Professional Learning Communities at Work and Virtual Collaboration: On the Tipping Point of Transformation,* by Richard DuFour and Casey Reason

- *Protocols for Professional Learning,* by Lois Brown Easton

- *The Relevant Educator: How Connectedness Empowers Learning,* by Tom Whitby and Steven W. Anderson

- *Transparency: How Leaders Create a Culture of Candor,* by Warren Bennis, Daniel Goleman, James O'Toole, and Patricia Ward Biederman

Web Resources

- Access lesson plans from other educators in BetterLesson's learning community at http://betterlesson.com

- BetterLesson's resources from master blended teachers at http://betterlesson.com/blended_learning

- BlendedED Update from The Learning Accelerator at http://learningaccelerator.org/blog

- Blended Learning and Technology in the Classroom from Catlin Tucker at http://catlintucker.com

- Blended Learning Universe, an online database of blended learning programs worldwide at http://www.blendedlearning.org/directory

- Character Lab's resources for educators, including lesson plans, videos, and posters at https://characterlab.org/tools/grit

- Concerted Chaos blog from Andrew Thomasson at www.concertedchaos.com

- The Edcamp Foundation's resources for Edcamp participants and organizers at www.edcamp.org

- Jerry Blumengarten's database of PLN resources for educators at https://cybraryman.com/pln.html

- The Learning Accelerator's database of blended and personalized learning strategies at http://learningaccelerator.org

- Survey to measure your grit at http://angeladuckworth.com/grit-scale

- Videos from the Teaching Channel spotlighting teacher collaboration at https://www.teachingchannel.org/deeper-learning-playlist-teaching-teams

Appendix E

Guide for Coaching and Supporting Blended Teachers

Mindsets

Understood, adopted, and committed to

Competency 1: New Vision for Teaching and Learning		
Standards	Questions to Guide Planning, Reflection, and Goal-Setting	Coaching Strategies
1A: **Shift from teacher-led instruction to student-centered learning** for the purposes of meeting individual needs and fostering engagement and motivation.	How can I include student choice and interests? How will students be active learners? How can I incorporate purposeful talk among learners? How will students use technology?	Model in classrooms and through videos. Observe classrooms with a focus on student-centered learning.
1B: **Value collaboration** with various stakeholders to enhance student learning.	Who can support teaching and learning in my classroom? With whom could my students connect to extend their learning opportunities?	Bring in others for collaborative planning. Connect teachers with external resources virtually and in person.
1C: **Create learning environments that are flexible and personalized**, dependent on real-time data, direct observation, and interaction with and feedback from students.	How might I reenvision this space? Where can I create flexible learning spaces? How can I involve students in redesigning the space?	Visit innovative spaces. Model flexible spaces in classrooms and other school areas.
1D: **Model a growth-orientation** toward learning for self and others.	What are my strengths? What can I improve? How can I foster a growth mindset in students? What language can I use to model a growth mindset?	Model growth mindset. Share articles, books, and resources for teachers and students.
1E: Have an entrepreneurial spirit, and possess **creativity, imagination, and drive**.	What classroom procedure, concept, or idea can I approach in a different way?	Provide time and space for play and exploration.

Competency 2: Orientation Toward Change and Improvement		
Standards	**Questions to Guide Planning, Reflection, and Goal-Setting**	**Coaching Strategies**
2A: **Embrace change** and model this for others.	What is not working well and how can I improve it? What new technique have I learned about but not tried?	Be transparent about change for improvement. Celebrate change.
2B: Proactively **initiate change in response to students' needs** and progress.	According to data on student learning, what changes are needed? What practice do I need to add, change, or remove?	Assist with data analysis. Brainstorm changes to address learning needs.
2C: **Embrace uncertainty and ambiguity** as part of improving teacher and learning practices.	What am I wondering about my students? What is unclear? Who can help me see what I may be missing?	Observe and provide honest feedback.
2D: **Model** and encourage others to be **independent and self-directed learners**.	What are my personal and professional learning needs and interests? What resources and tools can I use to learn?	Model and provide opportunities for self-directed learning.
2E: Demonstrate the professional responsibility to **contribute to the effectiveness, innovation, vitality, and self-renewal of the teaching profession**, as well as to their [teachers'] **school** and **community**.	How can I share what I am learning? How might my teaching practices affect the teaching of others? What do I need to share with my colleagues?	Model and provide opportunities for contributing to the school, community, and profession.

Qualities

Coached, encouraged, and reinforced

Competency 1: Grit		
Standards	**Questions to Guide Planning, Reflection, and Goal-Setting**	**Coaching Strategies**
1A: Engage in deliberate practice and **persevere toward ambitious, long-term educational and professional goals**.	What are my professional learning goals? What is my plan for accomplishing those goals? How can I share my goals with others? How might I overcome potential roadblocks and challenges?	Model perseverance toward goals. Assist with development of professional learning plans.
1B: Maintain and **model persistence, confidence, and optimism to resolve issues**.	What current challenge am I facing? What resources and strategies are available? How can I help others resolve issues?	Collaborate in problem solving. Celebrate small wins.

Competency 2: Transparency		
Standards	Questions to Guide Planning, Reflection, and Goal-Setting	Coaching Strategies
2A: Openly and frequently **share successes, failures, and challenges**.	What is working well and what isn't? How can I share my failures and successes with students and colleagues?	Create and facilitate opportunities for celebration.
2B: **Look objectively at all results** (both positive and negative), and help others to do the same.	What do the data reveal? What might I be missing in my data analysis? How can I help colleagues analyze results?	Facilitate data analysis. Provide objective feedback.

Competency 3: Collaboration		
Standards	Questions to Guide Planning, Reflection, and Goal-Setting	Coaching Strategies
3A: **Balance individual initiative with teamwork** to accomplish organizational objectives.	What goals is my team working toward? What is my role in helping the team meet those goals? What can I contribute?	Model individual initiative and teamwork. Facilitate goal-setting.
3B: Proactively **seek to learn from and with other experts** in the field.	What face-to-face and online opportunities are available to learn from and alongside other educators?	Provide opportunities to teach and learn from others.

Adaptive Skills

Developed through modeling, coaching, and reflective practice

Competency 1: Reflection		
Standards	Questions to Guide Planning, Reflection, and Goal-Setting	Coaching Strategies
1A: Continuously **take note of what is or is not working** (via student-level data, technology applications, pedagogical strategies, supervisor feedback, etc.) and **identify a plan of action**.	What do the data reveal about progress toward student learning goals? What data sources am I using? What additional data sources may be available? What should I celebrate? What are areas for improvement? What strategies can I implement to address those needs?	Facilitate data analysis. Provide data through observations and feedback. Assist with development of action plans.
1B: Collaboratively, transparently, and **proactively seek out feedback from students, parents, and colleagues** to continuously improve instruction and teaching practices.	How can I gather feedback on my teaching? Whose input do I currently have? What perspectives are missing?	Provide feedback on teaching practices. Create opportunities for collaborative feedback.

(Continued)

(Continued)

Competency 1: Reflection		
Standards	**Questions to Guide Planning, Reflection, and Goal-Setting**	**Coaching Strategies**
1C: **Apply lessons and takeaways about their** [teachers'] **own experiences as learners**, both online and offline, to their work with students.	How can my own learning experiences affect my instruction? What works for me as a learner? How might I use that in my teaching?	Provide professional learning opportunities and encourage teacher reflection.

Competency 2: Continuous Improvement and Innovation		
Standards	**Questions to Guide Planning, Reflection, and Goal-Setting**	**Coaching Strategies**
2A: Engage in **problem solving through continuous planning, designing, testing, evaluation, and recalibration** of teaching methods.	What new or revised teaching method have you used? What new or revised teaching method might you try? How have you/can you gather data to determine their effectiveness?	Teach and model the design process as a way to design and test innovative teaching methods.
2B: **Use technology creatively and purposefully** to work effectively and efficiently.	What technologies do you use to increase productivity, effectiveness, and efficiency? What process could you improve through technology?	Model creative and purposeful uses of technology. Provide professional learning.

Competency 3: Communication		
Standards	**Questions to Guide Planning, Reflection, and Goal-Setting**	**Coaching Strategies**
3A: **Connect learners to sources of information** beyond the classroom, teacher, and textbook.	What sources of information do students have access to at school and outside school? How can I design learning opportunities to leverage those sources?	Assist with development, curation, and evaluation of digital content.
3B: **Establish and maintain open communication channels**, online and in-person, with students, educators, and other stakeholders to support student learning.	What face-to-face and online communication channels do I and can I use with students, families, colleagues, and others? How can I leverage online communication for student learning?	Model effective in-person and online communication. Assist with school-wide communication.

Technical Skills

Acquired and mastered through instruction, training, and practice

Competency 1: Data Practices		
Standards	Questions to Guide Planning, Reflection, and Goal-Setting	Coaching Strategies
1A: **Use qualitative and quantitative data** to understand individual skills, gaps, strengths, weaknesses, interests, and aspirations of each student, and **use that information to personalize learning experiences**.	How do you gather ongoing data about student strengths, gaps, interests, and goals? How do you use that data to personalize learning experiences? What additional data sources might you use?	Model personalized learning for teachers. Facilitate data analysis. Assist with development of data collection plans.
1B: **Continually assess student progress against clearly defined standards, goals, and outcomes** to identify specific topics in which each student needs additional support to achieve mastery of a concept or skill.	How do you determine goals for student learning? How do you communicate those goals with students? What data do you use to assess progress toward those goals?	Facilitate goal-setting and data analysis. Assist with development of personalized learning plans for students.
1C: **Use data from multiple sources**, including data systems, in a complementary way to **inform and adjust individual student instruction and groupings**.	What do the data reveal about student learning? What are the learning needs of specific students and groups of students? How do I and can I use flexible grouping?	Assist with locating data sources and analyzing data. Model the use of data for flexible grouping.
1D: Create ways to **move ownership and analysis of data to students** to promote independent learning.	How are students involved in data collection and goal-setting? How do I share data about student learning with students? How can I move ownership of data to students?	Assist with data notebooking and student-led conferencing.
1E: **Continually evaluate technologies, tools, and instructional strategies** to ensure their effectiveness.	How do I determine the effectiveness of strategies and tools? Which strategies and tools are working and which are not?	Create and facilitate processes for ongoing evaluation of strategies and tools.
Competency 2: Instructional Strategies		
Standards	Questions to Guide Planning, Reflection, and Goal-Setting	Coaching Strategies
2A: Provide resources for students to learn content and **enable them to work independently and/or in cooperative groups**.	How do I use the learning management system to provide content? In what ways do students work independently and cooperatively? What new opportunities might I create for independent and collaborative learning?	Provide professional learning for instructional design. Assist with designing collaborative learning opportunities.

(Continued)

(Continued)

Competency 2: Instructional Strategies		
Standards	**Questions to Guide Planning, Reflection, and Goal-Setting**	**Coaching Strategies**
2B: Provide resources for students to **create evidence of their knowledge in a variety of formats** to demonstrate mastery.	How do students show what they know? How might I provide choice in how students show what they know?	Create a database of student work samples as a model for teachers.
2C: **Create customized learning pathways with students**, where learning goals and objectives are linked to explicit and diverse learning experiences, matched to the individual student's learning performance level and preferences.	How is learning personalized for students? What is the role of students in developing individualized learning pathways? How can I create new, diverse pathways linked to individual students' learning needs and goals?	Model use of individualized learning pathways for teachers. Assist with development of customized learning pathways for students.
2D: **Tailor content and instructional strategies to individual learning goals, needs, and interests**.	How are my instructional strategies matched to student learning needs, goals, and interests? How might I add more variety to my instructional strategies?	Share instructional strategies. Provide feedback from classroom observations.
2E: Create pedagogical approaches and learning experiences that **promote content-based problem solving and online collaboration**.	How often do my students engage in face-to-face and online collaborative problem solving? How might I use project-based learning to promote authentic problem solving and collaboration?	Share technologies that support online collaboration. Facilitate collaborative planning to design project-based learning challenges.
2F: **Develop and deliver valid and reliable assessments, projects, and assignments that meet standards-based criteria** and assess learning progress by measuring student achievement of learning goals.	How do I ensure alignment between standards and assessments, projects, and assignments? In what ways do I measure student learning according to standards? How can I better measure student achievement of learning goals?	Assist with development of valid and reliable assessments, projects, and assignments that are aligned with standards.
Competency 3: Management of Blended Learning Experience		
Standards	**Questions to Guide Planning, Reflection, and Goal-Setting**	**Coaching Strategies**
3A: Understand and **manage the face-to-face and online components of lesson planning** and organization within a blended course.	What model of blended learning do I currently use? What management challenges do I face? How can I better manage face-to-face and online instruction?	Share tools and processes for managing face-to-face and online instruction.
3B: Provide balanced opportunities for students to participate in **asynchronous and synchronous modalities**.	What synchronous and asynchronous tools would work well with my learners? How might I use them to provide opportunities for online discussions?	Model the use of synchronous and asynchronous tools.

Competency 3: Management of Blended Learning Experience		
Standards	**Questions to Guide Planning, Reflection, and Goal-Setting**	**Coaching Strategies**
3C: **Develop, practice, model, and embody respectful behaviors** in both face-to-face and online learning environments.	How do you model and explicitly teach respectful behaviors face-to-face and online? What specific behaviors do your students need to learn?	Model respectful behaviors in face-to-face and online environments.
3D: **Demonstrate technical troubleshooting** skills during the online component of learning (e.g., change passwords, download plug-ins, etc.).	What potential technical difficulties may pose a challenge during online instruction? How can I proactively address those challenges?	Model technical troubleshooting.
Competency 4: Instructional Tools		
Standards	**Questions to Guide Planning, Reflection, and Goal-Setting**	**Coaching Strategies**
4A: **Use learning management system and/or other online collaborative tools** to organize and manage the blended learning environment.	How am I currently using the learning management system and other online collaborative tools? How can these tools help me manage blended learning? What tools do I need to learn and implement?	Model management of blended professional learning through the learning management system and other tools.
4B: Demonstrate skill in the **evaluation, selection, and use of effective instructional materials, tools, strategies, and resources for students**, and engage students in this process to help their achievement and development of academic skills.	How do I identify, evaluate, and use instructional strategies, materials, and tools? What should I consider when evaluating new strategies, materials, and tools? How can I involve students in this process?	Share vetted resources, strategies, and tools. Assist with development of criteria for evaluating resources, strategies, and tools.
4C: **Provide assistive technologies** to facilitate learning.	What current learning needs should I address through assistive technologies? What assistive technologies are available to me? What assistive technologies do students need that are not currently available?	Ensure access to assistive technologies as needed. Provide professional learning opportunities for teachers.

References

Bennis, W., Goleman, D., O'Toole, J., & Biederman, P. W. (2014). *Transparency: How leaders create a culture of candor.* San Francisco, CA: Jossey-Bass.

Child Development Project. (1996). *Ways we want our class to be: Class meetings that build commitment to kindness and learning.* Oakland, CA: Developmental Studies Center.

Couros, G. (2015). *The innovator's mindset: Empower learning, unleash talent, and lead a culture of creativity.* San Diego, CA: Dave Burgess Consulting.

Duckworth, A. (2017). *Grit: The power of passion and perseverance.* London, UK: Vermillion.

DuFour, R., DuFour, R., Eaker, R., & Many, T. (2006). *Learning by doing: A handbook for professional learning communities at work* (3rd ed.). Bloomington, IN: Solution Tree.

DuFour, R., & Reason, C. (2016). *Professional learning communities at work and virtual collaboration: On the tipping point of transformation.* Bloomington, IN: Solution Tree.

Dweck, C., Gavin, M., & Gildan Media Corp. (2011). *Mindset: The new psychology of success.* New York, NY: Gildan Media Corp.

Easton, L. B. (2009). *Protocols for professional learning.* Alexandria, VA: Association for Supervision and Curriculum Development.

Hallermann, S., Larmer, J., Mergendoller, J. R., & Buck Institute for Education. (2016). *PBL in the elementary grades: Step-by-step guidance, tools and tips for standards-focused K–5 projects.* Novato, CA: Buck Institute for Education.

Horn, M. B., & Staker, H. (2014). *Blended: Using disruptive innovation to improve schools.* San Francisco, CA: Jossey-Bass.

The International Association for K–12 Online Learning (iNACOL). (2014). *iNACOL Blended Learning Teacher Competencies Framework.* http://www.inacol.org/resource/inacol-blended-learning-teacher-competency-framework/

Mertler, C. A. (2017). *Action research: Improving schools and empowering educators* (5th ed.). Thousand Oaks, CA: Sage.

Patterson, K., Grenny, J., McMillan, R., Switzler, A., Covey, S. R., & Roppe, L. (2013). *Crucial conversations.* Grand Haven, MI: Brilliance Audio.

Tough, P. (2013). *How children succeed: Grit, curiosity, and the hidden power of character.* Boston, MA: Mariner Books, Houghton Mifflin Harcourt.

Webber, E. (2016). *Building successful communities of practice.* London, UK: Drew London.

Whitby, T., & Anderson, S. W. (2014). *The relevant educator: How connectedness empowers learning.* Thousand Oaks, CA: Corwin.

Index

Corwin books represent the latest thinking from some of the most respected experts in K–12 education. We are proud of the breadth and depth of the books we have published and the authors we have partnered with in our mission to better serve educators and students.

Barbara Bray, Kathleen McClaskey

Find tools, skills, and strategies needed to develop independent learners.

Barbara Bray, Kathleen McClaskey

Learn to implement strategies to guide students into becoming self-directed, self-monitoring, and self-motivated learners.

Julie Stern, Nathalie Lauriault, Krista Ferraro

Harness natural curiosity and keep your students asking questions with concept-based teaching methods.

James Nottingham

Dive into the learning pit and show students how to promote challenge, dialogue, and a growth mindset.

CORWIN
A SAGE Publishing Company

A SAGE Publishing Company

Helping educators make the greatest impact

CORWIN HAS ONE MISSION: to enhance education through intentional professional learning.

We build long-term relationships with our authors, educators, clients, and associations who partner with us to develop and continuously improve the best evidence-based practices that establish and support lifelong learning.

Solutions you want. Experts you trust.
Results you need.

AUTHOR CONSULTING

Author Consulting

On-site professional learning with sustainable results! Let us help you design a professional learning plan to meet the unique needs of your school or district. www.corwin.com/pd

INSTITUTES

Institutes

Corwin Institutes provide collaborative learning experiences that equip your team with tools and action plans ready for immediate implementation. www.corwin.com/institutes

eCOURSES

eCourses

Practical, flexible online professional learning designed to let you go at your own pace. www.corwin.com/ecourses

READ2EARN

Read2Earn

Did you know you can earn graduate credit for reading this book? Find out how: www.corwin.com/read2earn